NEW DIRECTIONS FOR EVALUATION
A Publication of the American Evaluation Association

Gary T. Henry, *Georgia State University*
EDITOR-IN-CHIEF

Jennifer C. Greene, *Cornell University*
EDITOR-IN-CHIEF

# Advances in Mixed-Method Evaluation: The Challenges and Benefits of Integrating Diverse Paradigms

Jennifer C. Greene
*Cornell University*

Valerie J. Caracelli
*U.S. General Accounting Office*

EDITORS

SO-BYX-072

Number 74, Summer 1997

JOSSEY-BASS PUBLISHERS
San Francisco

ADVANCES IN MIXED-METHOD EVALUATION: THE CHALLENGES AND
BENEFITS OF INTEGRATING DIVERSE PARADIGMS
*Jennifer C. Greene, Valerie J. Caracelli* (eds.)
New Directions for Evaluation, no. 74
*Jennifer C. Greene, Gary T. Henry,* Editors-in-Chief

*New Directions for Evaluation* is indexed in Contents Pages in Education,
Higher Education Abstracts, and Sociological Abstracts.

Microfilm copies of issues and articles are available in 16mm and 35mm,
as well as microfiche in 105mm, through University Microfilms Inc., 300
North Zeeb Road, Ann Arbor, Michigan 48106-1346.

ISSN 0164-7989        ISBN 0-7879-9822-2

NEW DIRECTIONS FOR EVALUATION is part of The Jossey-Bass Education
Series and is published quarterly by Jossey-Bass Inc., Publishers, 350
Sansome Street, San Francisco, California 94104-1342.

Subscriptions cost $63.00 for individuals and $105.00 for institutions,
agencies, and libraries. Prices subject to change.

EDITORIAL CORRESPONDENCE should be addressed to the Editors-in-Chief,
Jennifer C. Greene, Department of Human Service Studies, Cornell University, Ithaca, NY 14853-4401, or Gary T. Henry, Public Administration
and Urban Studies, Georgia State University, Atlanta, GA 30302-4039.

Jossey-Bass Web address: http://www.josseybass.com

Manufactured in the United States of America on Lyons Falls
Turin Book. This paper is acid-free and 100 percent totally
chlorine-free.

# EDITORIAL POLICY AND PROCEDURES

*New Directions for Evaluation,* a quarterly sourcebook, is an official publication of the American Evaluation Association. The journal publishes empirical, methodological, and theoretical works on all aspects of evaluation. A reflective approach to evaluation is an essential strand to be woven through every volume. The editors encourage volumes that have one of three foci: (1) craft volumes that present approaches, methods, or techniques that can be applied in evaluation practice, such as the use of templates, case studies, or survey research; (2) professional issue volumes that present issues of import for the field of evaluation, such as utilization of evaluation or locus of evaluation capacity; (3) societal issue volumes that draw out the implications of intellectual, social, or cultural developments for the field of evaluation, such as the women's movement, communitarianism, or multiculturalism. A wide range of substantive domains is appropriate for *New Directions for Evaluation;* however, the domains must be of interest to a large audience within the field of evaluation. We encourage a diversity of perspectives and experiences within each volume, as well as creative bridges between evaluation and other sectors of our collective lives.

The editors do not consider or publish unsolicited single manuscripts. Each issue of the journal is devoted to a single topic, with contributions solicited, organized, reviewed, and edited by a guest editor. Issues may take any of several forms, such as a series of related chapters, a debate, or a long article followed by brief critical commentaries. In all cases, the proposals must follow a specific format, which can be obtained from the editor-in-chief. These proposals are sent to members of the editorial board and to relevant substantive experts for peer review. The process may result in acceptance, a recommendation to revise and resubmit, or rejection. However, the editors are committed to working constructively with potential guest editors to help them develop acceptable proposals.

Jennifer C. Greene, Editor-in-Chief
Department of Policy Analysis and Management
MVR Hall
Cornell University
Ithaca, NY 14853
email: jcg8@cornell.edu

Gary T. Henry, Editor-in-Chief
School of Policy Studies
Georgia State University
P.O. Box 4039
Atlanta, GA 30302–4039
e-mail: gthenry@gsu.edu

# Contents

# Editors' Notes

Evaluation theory and practice today are characteristically pluralistic, embracing diverse perspectives, methods, data, and values within and across studies that aim to generate more insightful and meaningful evaluative claims. This volume seeks to strengthen the promise of pluralistic evaluation by advancing an enhanced conceptual framework for planning and implementing mixed-method evaluation studies. Previous mixed-method work has concentrated on the technical level of method, focusing on combining qualitative and quantitative methods within one evaluation study. The present mixed-method volume addresses the philosophical level of paradigm, analyzing the challenges of combining in one study different, even conflicting, assumptions about the nature of social phenomena and our claims to know them.

The first two chapters of this volume, which we the editors wrote, outline and respond to these challenges both conceptually and practically. In Chapter One, we frame the current mixed-method conversation as three primary stances on the sensibleness of mixing paradigms while mixing methods in evaluative inquiry. These positions include: (1) the *purist* stance, in which people argue against mixing paradigms; (2) the *pragmatic* stance, in which people view paradigms as useful conceptual constructions but base practical methodological decisions on contextual responsiveness and relevance, thereby often including diverse methods; and (3) the *dialectical* stance, in which people view paradigms as important guides for practice and regard the inevitable tensions invoked by juxtaposing different paradigms as potentially generating more complete, more insightful, even transformed evaluative understandings.

We then critique these stances and argue for a shift in the mixed-method conversation. Such a shift would be away from a preoccupation with explicit assumptive differences between paradigms, such as objectivity-subjectivity and realism-relativism, and toward other characteristics of social inquiry traditions. These must be characteristics that define inquiry traditions in important ways and therefore warrant our attention and respect but that are also not logically irreconcilable when juxtaposed with contrasting characteristics. Examples offered in Chapter One emphasize critical features of the knowledge claims generated by different paradigmatic traditions (for example, distance and closeness, particularity and generality) and the different values and interests that various traditions advance. The significant idea here is to redirect the bases for mixing methods away from what may well be incommensurable philosophical assumptions and toward other inquiry characteristics that can more productively share a common analytic space.

In Chapter Two, we first highlight the work of George Julnes as a fine example of an integrative perspective (emergent critical realism) that productively focuses on specific features of different inquiry traditions, notably, deduction

1

versus induction and molar versus molecular causality. We then offer our own practical ideas about two main classes of mixed-method, mixed-paradigm design alternatives that can productively combine critical features of different traditions. The first is *component* designs, in which the different methods remain discrete throughout the inquiry so that they are combined at the level of interpretation and inference. Three specific examples of component designs that build directly from our earlier work on mixed-method purposes are triangulation, complementarity, and expansion. The second class of *integrated* mixed-method designs attains greater integration of the different method types during the inquiry and analytic processes. Specific examples of integrated designs, which are illustrated and discussed in Chapter Two, include iterative, embedded or nested, holistic, and transformative designs. While we believe that mixed-method component designs are more likely to be implemented within a pragmatic stance and that integrative designs are more likely to offer dialectical potential, these are descriptive linkages, not prescriptions.

In the next four chapters of this volume, these conceptual and practical ideas about mixing methods and paradigms are further explored and expanded using the primary vehicle of case studies. In Chapter Three, Lois-ellin Datta refines and augments the pragmatist stance by offering three specific pragmatic criteria for choosing methods—practicality, contextual responsiveness, and consequentiality—which she also frames as four specific questions to ask about the practical consequences of design decisions. Answers to these questions lead to two situations in which a mixed-method design would be chosen: (1) "satisficing," in which a mixed-method design will reasonably substitute for the preferred, but not possible, mono-method design; and (2) "better-than," in which a mixed-method design is the best or only way to go. Datta then illustrates these different situations with case examples.

In Chapter Four, Melvin M. Mark, Irwin Feller, and Scott B. Button richly illuminate pragmatic and dialectical, as well as component and integrative, design features in their detailed analysis of a complex mixed-method evaluation study that incorporated qualitative methods within a predominantly quantitative design. They persuasively argue that classifying a mixed-method strand of a study as either pragmatic or dialectical depends significantly on what actually happens in practice rather than only on intent. As they observe, "Productive dialectics sometimes occur and sometimes do not." These authors also challenge the paradigmatic anchors around which this volume was developed. Noting that paradigms are but social constructions, they advocate not a continued reliance on old paradigms but rather the development of a new paradigm (specifically, emergent realism) that inherently embraces multiple methods and integrative knowledge claims.

In Chapter Five, Huey-tsyh Chen vigorously rejects the idea of developing a new, mixed-method paradigm, and argues instead for a contextualized, contingent conceptualization of what matters in mixed-method designs. Chen then offers two case studies, both conducted within his (holistic) framework of theory-driven evaluation. Chen's evaluation of a garbage-reduction intervention in Taiwan is a fine example of a component design. As detailed in his own analysis, Chen's evaluation of an anti–drug abuse program in Taiwan illustrates well the potential value of integrative, holistic, mixed-method designs.

Mary Lee Smith's highly instructive mixed-method case example in Chapter Six is framed by her view that what best guides evaluation practice is not abstract philosophical paradigms but evaluators' "crude mental models" of what the world and evaluation are like. Smith then offers portraits of three mental models and the method-mixing practices that follow from them. Her case study is grounded in Mental Model III, which is centered around phenomenological knowing but does not privilege any particular method or data form. Like the Chapter Four authors, Smith challenges the paradigm construct we used for our arguments in Chapters One and Two, and offers an integrative alternative. Interestingly, we see Smith's alternative—her Mental Model III—as grounded primarily in interpretive assumptions, and the Chapter Four authors' alternative—the paradigm of emergent realism—as grounded primarily in postpositivist assumptions, even though both alternatives help shift and reframe the mixed-method conversation in more generative and productive directions.

Finally, in Chapter Seven, Leslie J. C. Riggin offers an independent analysis and critique of the entire volume. She links the case studies offered in Chapters Three through Six to our conceptual and practical ideas in Chapters One and Two. Her discussion provides a critical synthesis of the ways in which the ideas in this volume actually advance the mixed-method conversation.

Jennifer C. Greene
Valerie J. Caracelli
Editors

JENNIFER C. GREENE is associate professor of human service studies at Cornell University. Her evaluation work concentrates on qualitative, participatory, and mixed-method approaches.

VALERIE J. CARACELLI is senior social science analyst at the U.S. General Accounting Office.

*Current stances on mixing methods and paradigms are described and
critiqued. Ideas are offered for advancing mixed-method evaluation
beyond age-worn paradigm debates.*

# Defining and Describing the Paradigm Issue in Mixed-Method Evaluation

*Jennifer C. Greene, Valerie J. Caracelli*

This is an era of methodological pluralism in applied social science, including
the field of evaluation. Multiple frameworks for inquiry abound. Interpretivist,
postpositivist, activist, literary, feminist, and critical frameworks, among others, compete for our attention and allegiance. The dissonance and discord created by such competition (see Lincoln, 1991; Sechrest, 1992) are softened, to
a degree, by continuing endeavors to embrace multiple methodologies within
the same study or the same inquiry project (among many other works, see
Brewer and Hunter, 1989; Bryman, 1988; Cook, 1985; Firestone, 1990; Fishman, 1991; Howe, 1985, 1988; Mark and Shotland, 1987; Maxwell, 1996;
Reichardt and Rallis, 1994; Shadish, 1995). The work presented in this volume supports and advances these endeavors. Indeed, its premise is that using
multiple and diverse methods is a good idea, but is not automatically good science. Rather, just as survey research, quasi-experimentation, panel studies, and
case studies require careful planning and thoughtful decisions, so do mixed-
method studies. Lacking justification and planning, mixed-method decisions
may not be defensible.

Yet, just what is required for planned, defensible mixed-method decisions in evaluative inquiry? As in other inquiry logics and frameworks, what
is required is thoughtful guidance at three important levels of inquiry decision making:

1. The political level, or the level of purpose, which encompasses the broad,
   value-based questions about the purpose and role of evaluation in society
2. The philosophical level, or the level of paradigm, which incorporates
   assumptions and stances about the social world and our ability to know it

New Directions for Evaluation, no. 74, Summer 1997 © Jossey-Bass Publishers

5

3. The technical level, or the level of method, which represents discrete methods and procedures for gathering and analyzing information

This issue concentrates on the second level—it takes on the "paradigm issue" in mixed-method evaluative inquiry. This volume sharply defines and analyzes the challenges involved in intentionally mixing methodologies that represent disparate philosophical paradigms and thus different, even conflicting, assumptions about the nature of social phenomena and our claims to know them. This first chapter outlines the contours of the often contentious debate on this paradigm issue and previews promising directions for evaluative inquiry that *does* incorporate dimensions of distinct paradigms meaningfully. Subsequent chapters develop these directions more fully.

While this volume concentrates on the issues involved in mixing paradigms, the discussion interweaves strands related to the other two levels of inquiry planning—the broad level of purpose and the specific level of method. This intertwinement is both intentional and inevitable, for these three levels of inquiry decision making are fully interconnected, both conceptually and practically. Although these questions about inquiry purpose and role broadly constitute a commanding debate within late twentieth-century social science, they have not significantly penetrated the mixed-method conversation. Thus, this conversation has been heretofore more technical than political and more philosophical than ideological. While not straying too far from technique and philosophy, this volume does take an initial, albeit small, step toward infusing the value and political dimensions of evaluative inquiry into the ongoing mixed-method conversation.

## Describing the "Paradigm Issue" in Mixed-Method Evaluation Inquiry

This chapter endeavors to describe, critique, and reframe the current mixed-method conversation. This section defines the core constructs involved.

**Defining the Terms.**  This chapter construes a social inquiry paradigm as a set of interlocking philosophical assumptions and stances about knowledge, our social world, our ability to know that world, and our reasons for knowing it—assumptions that collectively warrant certain methods, certain knowledge claims, and certain actions on those claims. A paradigm frames and guides a particular orientation to social inquiry, including what questions to ask, what methods to use, what knowledge claims to strive for, and what defines high-quality work (see Lincoln and Guba, 1985; Patton, 1990).

The mixed-method discussion within the evaluation community has been dominated to date by two paradigms—the interpretivist, or constructivist, paradigm (exemplified by Lincoln and Guba, 1985), and the postpositivist, or postempiricist, paradigm (exemplified by Campbell, 1969; Cook, 1985). These two paradigms have cornered much of the discourse, characteristically dubbed the *quantitative-qualitative debate*. Further, this debate has been cast largely in terms of the contrasting philosophical tenets and stances of these two paradigms, for example, realism versus relativism and objectivity versus subjectivity. As this chapter argues, recasting this debate in terms of other dimensions of evaluative claims may help advance the debate. While this chapter concentrates on these two paradigms, the logic of the discussion is meant to extend to other, diverse, social inquiry paradigms.

A method, then, is a procedure for gathering or analyzing data. Examples of methods include questionnaires, interviews, observations, and archival records, each of which can gather information that is quantifiable or that remains qualitative or symbolic. Methods are not intrinsically linked to any particular paradigm (Bednarz, 1985; Reichardt and Cook, 1979).

Mixed-method inquiry intentionally combines different methods—that is, methods meant to gather different kinds of information. For the mixed-method inquiry that is the focus of this chapter, the various methods *are* linked to different inquiry paradigms. The underlying premise of mixed-method inquiry is that each paradigm offers a meaningful and legitimate way of knowing and understanding. The underlying rationale for mixed-method inquiry is to understand more fully, to generate deeper and broader insights, to develop important knowledge claims that respect a wider range of interests and perspectives.

**Framing the Issue.** Currently, there is wide consensus that mixing different types of methods at the technical level, or the level of method, is not problematic and can often strengthen a given study. In fact, there are many logical and compelling reasons for intentionally using multiple, varied methods in applied social science. Different kinds of methods are best suited to learning about different kinds of phenomena. All methods have limitations and biases; using multiple methods can help to counteract some of these biases. (This is the classic argument for *triangulation* in both postpositivist [Campbell and Fiske, 1959; Cook, 1985] and interpretivist [Denzin, 1978] traditions.) All methods and claims to know are fallible; using multiple diverse methods helps to address this. Further, social phenomena are extremely complex, so different kinds of methods are needed to understand the important complexities of our social world more completely.

Substantial mixed-method work has been conducted at the technical level of method. Useful guidance for the mixed-method practitioner is available with respect to figuring out which aspects of a study to make multiple (Shotland and Mark, 1987), selecting specific mixed-method purposes and designs (Greene, Caracelli, and Graham, 1989; see also Creswell, 1994), choosing an appropriate mixed-method data analysis strategy (Caracelli and Greene, 1993), and identifying appropriate quality criteria for judging a mixed-method study (Riggin and Caracelli, 1994; see also Howe and Eisenhart, 1990).

The debate thus has raged and continues at least to simmer at the level of philosophy or paradigm. In this level, there are sharply discordant views on the wisdom, justifiability, and efficacy of mixing methods that *are* linked to different inquiry paradigms. These views are outlined in the next section.

## Three Stances on Mixing Paradigms in Mixed-Method Evaluation

Past work (Greene, Caracelli, and Graham, 1989; Kidder and Fine, 1987; Reichardt and Cook, 1979; Rossman and Wilson, 1985; Smith, 1994) shows that there are three primary stances on the sensibleness and efficacy of mixing paradigms while mixing methods in evaluative inquiry.

1. Proponents of the *purist* stance (Guba and Lincoln, 1989; Smith, 1983) argue that different inquiry frameworks or paradigms embody fundamentally different and incompatible assumptions about human nature, the world, the nature of knowledge claims, and what it is possible to know and, moreover, that these assumptions form an interconnected whole that cannot be meaningfully divided. Hence, it is neither possible nor sensible to mix different inquiry paradigms within a single study or project. Within the mixed-method conversation, this purist stance is retained primarily as a counterpoint to the remaining two stances, which *do* acknowledge the possibility—even the sensibleness—of mixing paradigms while mixing methods.

2. The *pragmatic* position also maintains that there are philosophical differences between various paradigms of inquiry. But, for the pragmatist, these philosophical assumptions are logically independent and therefore can be mixed and matched, in conjunction with choices about methods, to achieve the combination most appropriate for a given inquiry problem. Moreover, these paradigm differences do not really matter very much to the practice of social inquiry, because paradigms are best viewed as descriptions of, not prescriptions for, research practice. What is more important—and what should drive all methodological decisions in social inquiry—is the inquiry problem's practical demands. Inquirers, that is, should be able to choose what will "work best" for a given inquiry problem "without being limited or inhibited" (Patton, 1988, p. 117) by philosophical assumptions. Given the inherent complexity of social scientific problems—especially applied problems of the field, including all evaluation problems—what will work best is often a combination of different methods.

3. The *dialectical* position argues that differences between philosophical paradigms or logics of justification for social scientific inquiry not only exist but are important. These differences cannot be ignored or reconciled (as the legacy of historical dualisms has shown [Krantz, 1995]), but rather must be honored in ways that maintain the integrity of the disparate paradigms. Moreover, the differences should be deliberately used both within and across studies toward a dialectical discovery of enhanced understandings, of new and revisioned perspectives and meanings. Salomon (1991), for example, argues that social issues are vastly complex and thus require both an "analytic" and a "systemic" approach to inquiry, used complementarily across studies for a more complete understanding. Ragin (1989) maintains that comparative social inquiry can best be advanced via a synthesis of "case- and variable-oriented approaches." This synthesis "must be holistic—so that the cases themselves are

not lost in the research process—and analytic, so that more than a few cases can be comprehended and modest generalization is possible" (p. xiv).

Excluding the purist stance because it does not permit the possibility of mixing methods framed by different paradigms, we elaborate and illustrate the two primary mixed-method stances in the discussion that follows. We selected the illustrations for their heuristic value, so some represent fields other than evaluation.

**Being Pragmatic: The Position.** Michael Patton (1988) is a leading proponent of the pragmatic position. Here are the specific points in his argument.

1. Paradigm differences are real in that "they describe much research practice" (Patton, 1988, p. 118). Interpretivists typically use qualitative methods, postpositivists typically use quantitative methods, and these two types of studies typically vary along such dimensions as induction-deduction and context specificity–generalizability.

2. Such distinctions and linkages are not logically required, however, and therefore need not be prescribed. Rather, "The purpose of describing alternative research paradigms is to sensitize researchers and evaluators to the ways in which their methodological prejudices, derived from their disciplinary socialization experiences, may reduce their methodological flexibility and adaptability. The purpose of describing how paradigms typically operate in the real world is to free evaluators from the bonds of allegiance to a single paradigm" (Patton, 1988, p. 118).

3. Moreover, descriptions of alternative paradigms represent ideal types that contrast opposing ends of what are actually methodological continua, for example, objectivity-subjectivity. "Seldom do actual studies exemplify all the ideal characteristics of either paradigm. There is a lot of real world space between the ideal-typical endpoints of paradigmatic conceptualization" (Patton, 1988, p. 113).

4. Finally, even if one acknowledges that different paradigms contain incompatible assumptions, "pragmatism can overcome [such] seemingly logical contradictions" (Patton, 1988, p. 127). This is true because pragmatism does not require that any such contradictions be resolved before one uses diverse methodologies, but rather grounds its rationale for mixing methods in situational responsiveness and a commitment to an empirical perspective.

**A Pragmatic Example.** Willenbring and Spicer (1991) used both quantitative and qualitative methods in their evaluation of an intensive case management program for homeless, chemically dependent men. Drawing on billing statements and case records as data sources, Willenbring and Spicer used quantitative methods to analyze program clients' use of services. The qualitative methods assessed both client and staff program experiences and included interviews, participant observation, and detailed case studies. The authors clearly articulate the pragmatist stance of their study: "Our project sought to compare the effects of different intensities of case management, and we adopted a number of different qualitative and quantitative methods to do so. It is important to emphasize that we did so without considered analysis of epistemology or scientific typologies. Rather, we did so to maximize the amount of information we would gain and to strengthen our overall evaluation" (p. 2).

**Being Dialectical: The Position.** A *synergistic* approach to mixed-method inquiry reflects this stance well and is captured clearly by such evocative concepts as "double hermeneutics" (Giddens, 1976), "dialectical tacking" (Geertz, 1979), "weaving back and forth" (Fielding and Fielding, 1986; Rowles and Reinharz, 1987), and "shifting frames of reference" (Phelan, 1987). All refer to using methods shaped by both interpretivist and postpositivist paradigms in an integrative manner to generate more comprehensive, insightful, and logical results than either paradigm could obtain alone. The rationale for mixing methods in this stance is to understand more fully by generating new insights, in contrast to the pragmatic rationale of understanding more fully by being situationally responsive and relevant.

For example, Giddens's "double hermeneutic" process (1976) requires working back and forth between the scientific vocabulary of social science and the natural, everyday language of social life. Geertz (1979) argues for a continuous "dialectical tacking" between experience-near (particular, context-specific, idiographic) and experience-distant (general, universal, nomothetic) concepts, because both types of concepts are needed for comprehensive and meaningful understanding.

**Examples of Dialectical Inquiry.** Phelan's study of incest in the United States (1987) illustrates a *spiraled* combination of ethnographic and quantitative methods. An extended period of participant observation and in-depth interviewing in a treatment program yielded several working hypotheses about the differential form and meaning of incestual behavior for fathers and stepfathers.

These hypotheses were pursued via a quantitative analysis of information drawn from 102 cases. This analysis supported the preliminary hypothesis that the form of incest varied in structurally different families. For example, compared with stepfathers, natural fathers were more likely to be involved with multiple daughters and to have full intercourse. Phelan comments: "The results are striking. But, they are also sterile unless they are interwoven with possible meanings and interpretations of the events found in the qualitative analysis" (p. 39).

A return to the qualitative data for such interpretation indicated, for example, that stepfathers more often viewed their relationships with their stepdaughters as love affairs, warranting appropriate courtship behavior. In contrast, natural fathers were more likely to view their daughters as possessions, providing an interchangeable pool from which to satisfy their needs. The results of this study precipitated important changes in the treatment program, which theretofore had not differentiated family type in its treatment philosophy.

Methodologically, Phelan (1987, p. 41) underscored the significance of her mixed-method approach: "This is not a case of simply supplementing one methodology with another, but rather an example of having to move back and forth in order to begin to understand a sensitive area of human behavior."

In sociology, Fielding and Fielding (1986) note that qualitative fieldwork focuses on the microlevel of individual action (or action attributable to individual beliefs), while quantitative inquiry addresses the macrolevel of collective structure (or action governed by universal laws). Arguing that these micro- and macrolevels are integrated in daily life and that each "bears within it indirect reference to the existence of the other" (pp. 20–21), Fielding and Fielding assert that "an intimate 'back-and-forth,' testing, critique, and synthesis" of the two approaches stand "the best chance of specifying powerful solutions" to important inquiry problems (pp. 12–13).

## Critiquing These Mixed-Method Stances: Probing Underlying Issues

These varied stances on the paradigm issue in mixed-method social inquiry underscore the richness and depth of the mixed-method conversation. Especially in their extreme form, however, these stances also convey hardened positions that are difficult to reconfigure or redirect. The potential promise of mixed-method inquiry is not likely to be fulfilled from such hardened positions. To move toward such fulfillment, we will now analyze two of the issues underlying these varied mixed-method stances: (1) What is the appropriate relationship between inquiry paradigms and inquiry practice in evaluation and (2) Which characteristics of an inquiry paradigm matter in mixed-method evaluation practice? With this analysis, we hope to help shift the mixed-method conversation to more generative and integrative levels.

*What is the appropriate relationship between inquiry paradigms and inquiry practice in evaluation?* Adherents of the pragmatic position clearly reject the extremist stance of the purists, and appropriately so, in our view. Inquiry paradigms are only social constructions, just historically and culturally embedded discourse practices (Cherryholmes, 1988), and are therefore neither inviolate nor unchanging. The evolution of hermeneutics (Smith, 1989) and its postpositivist counterpoints—for example, Cook's critical multiplism (1985) and Campbell's coherentism (1991)—illustrate this point well. The purist position that inquiry paradigms prescribe practical decisions and dictate inquiry designs and method choices is not substantiated by this historical view of paradigms.

However, the pragmatists, especially the extremists in that camp, may err in granting too little authority to paradigms as shaping practical inquiry decisions. While the demands of the inquiry context are important, they may be insufficient guides for evaluative inquiry. Defensible practice also requires a set of assumptions and ideals about the social world, about the role of social knowledge claims in this world, and about oneself as a social inquirer—in other words, the framework provided by an inquiry paradigm. In addition to context, "methodology also depends on ontological and epistemological assumptions about the nature of reality and best ways of gaining access to that reality, so that knowledge about it can be formulated" (House, 1994, p. 15). Without this assumptive framework, the inquirer is perhaps too readily buffeted by the sociopolitical influences of the context. Responding with integrity, meaningfulness, and coherence to such influences requires a paradigmatic anchor.

Yet one must also be careful to eschew the tyranny "of the epistemological over the practical, of the conceptual over the empirical" and to insist "that paradigms bring themselves into some reasonable state of equilibrium with methods . . . such that practice is neither static and unreflective nor subject to the one-way dictates of a wholly abstract paradigm" (Howe, 1988, p. 13). Extremists within the dialectical stance may also err in granting too little authority to the inquiry context as shaping practical inquiry decisions.

The middle position here consists of a balanced, reciprocal relationship between philosophy and methodology, between paradigms and practice. This position rejects extremism in all of the mixed-method stances above, honors both the integrity of the paradigm construct and the legitimacy of contextual demands, and seeks a respectful, dialogical interaction between the two in guiding and shaping evaluation decisions in the field.

*Which characteristics of an inquiry paradigm matter in mixed-method evaluation practice?* Richard Bernstein (1993, p. 65) says that in this era of unprecedented paradigm proliferation, our task is "to assume the responsibility to listen carefully, to use our linguistic, emotional, and cognitive imagination to grasp what is being expressed and said in 'alien' traditions. We must do this in a way where we resist the dual temptations of either facilely assimilating what others are saying in our own categories and language without doing justice to what is genuinely different and may be incommensurable or simply dismissing what the 'other' is saying as incoherent nonsense."

Given this image of listening carefully to the "other," the question now becomes, What should we listen for? What should these conversations on paradigmatic differences be about? And, by extension for the present purposes, What is most important to mix in mixed-method evaluative inquiry? *What are the critical features of different inquiry traditions that, although likely to present tensions when combined, are important to preserve because they vitally define those traditions?*

We suggest that these mixed-method conversations should *not* continue to be preoccupied with the explicit assumptive differences between paradigms that have been frequently offered as points of contrast, conflict, and incompatibility. For interpretivism and postpositivism, these differences include: subjectivity-objectivity, induction-deduction, relativism-realism, holism-reductionism, monism-dualism. These are historical differences, which many still view as incommensurable and unlikely to be reconciled in our lifetimes (Bernstein, 1993; Krantz, 1995). Most prior mixed-method conversations have become stuck here.

Instead, we propose that the mixed-method conversation shift to other characteristics of social inquiry traditions. These must be characteristics that constitute important facets of inquiry traditions and therefore warrant our attention and respect but that are also not logically irreconcilable when juxtaposed with contrasting characteristics. Contrasts, conflicts, and tensions between different methods and their findings are an expected, even welcome dimension of mixed-method inquiry, for it is in the tension that the boundaries of what is known are most generatively challenged and stretched. The analytic space created by the tension, however, must offer the possibility of coordination, integration, and synthesis. To this, the constitutive characteristics must be other than irreconcilable philosophical assumptions.

One such promising alternative set of characteristics is the critical features of the knowledge claims generated by different paradigmatic traditions. For interpretivism and postpositivism, examples of such features include:

- Particularity and generality
- Closeness and distance
- Meaning and causality
- The unusual and the representative
- The diversity within the range and the central tendency of the mean
- Social constructions and physical traces
- Micro- and macrolenses, or setting and structure perspectives
- Integrative synthesis and componential analysis
- Insider and outside viewpoints (House, 1994)
- *Phronesis* and *episteme,* or practical wisdom and expert knowledge (Kessels and Korthagen, 1996)
- The contextualized understanding of local meanings and the distancing analysis of regularities

These represent characteristically different facets of knowledge claims generated from the different inquiry traditions of interpretivism and postpositivism—different, but not necessarily logically incompatible. A mixed-method study that combines these two traditions would strive for knowledge claims that are grounded in the lives of the participants studied and that also have some generality to other participants and other contexts, that enhance understanding of both the unusual and the typical case, that isolate factors of particular significance while also integrating the whole, that are full of emic meaning at the same time as they offer causal connections of broad significance. Compared with knowledge claims produced in a single-method study, this multiplistic, mixed-method set of knowledge claims is likely to be more pragmatically relevant and useful, and more dialectically insightful and generative, even if accompanied by unresolved tensions.

A second alternative set of characteristics of social inquiry paradigms that may productively advance the mixed-method conversation includes the different values and interests advocated by different methodological traditions. For example, postpositivism characteristically advances values of efficiency and utilitarianism; interpretivism typically promotes values of diversity and community. Postpositivist evaluations characteristically address the information needs and concerns of responsible decision makers; interpretivist evaluations generally focus on the concerns and issues of stakeholders closer to the program, including program staff and participants.

To listen carefully to "other" views on such matters, as encouraged by Bernstein (1993), is to reorient the mixed-method conversation—away from preoccupations with philosophy and methodology and toward questions of inquiry purpose and role in society. Such questions of purpose and role encompass diverse value claims and stances on legitimate knowledge, advocacy, action, and morality (Schwandt, 1996).

In this type of mixed-method conversation, methods are mixed in order to represent a *plurality* of interests, voices, and perspectives better. That is, the value-based and action-oriented dimensions of different inquiry traditions become the grounds on which methods and analysis decisions are made. These grounds, and therefore the decisions, are unavoidably *pluralistic,* mirroring the value and political pluralism of the larger society. This mixed-method conversation therefore offers opportunities for dialoguing across differences constituted by values and ideologies. Clearly, this would be a challenging and contentious conversation, but one that still offers greater promise of rapprochement than yet another debate on subjectivity versus objectivity.

There are still other related ideas for reframing the mixed-method conversation around inquiry characteristics that can meaningfully and generatively share the same analytic space. Some of these ideas are presented and discussed in this volume, including:

- The consequential or action dimensions of inquiry traditions, such that the mixed-method rationale of understanding more fully means generating more influential and inclusive action consequences (see Datta in Chapter Three of this volume)
- The specific roles and contributions that methods in one inquiry tradition offer methods in another, such that the better understanding attained via mixing methods means more warranted, defensible evaluative claims and inferences (see Mark, Feller, and Button in Chapter Four of this volume)
- The nature and role of substantive or program theory in different inquiry traditions, such that better understanding through mixed-method inquiry means a more complete, well-developed, defensible, and coherent program theory (see Chen in Chapter Five of this volume)
- Evaluators' own presumptive, nonformalized "mental models" of the social world they endeavor to know, such that better understanding through mixing methods means a more open, flexible, contingent mental model (see Smith in Chapter Six of this volume)

Better understanding does not require the prior resolution of epistemological or ontological debates about our social worlds. The significant idea here is to redirect the bases for mixing methods—away from what may well be incommensurable philosophical assumptions and toward other inquiry characteristics that can more productively share a common analytic space.

## Reprise

"The . . . constructivists [maintain] that since realities are multiple, truth relative, and accounts equally true or false, the best we as evaluators can do is to produce journalistic accounts. [This stance] begs the question of rigor and rationality. . . . It is an escape from responsibility and action. . . . The [post]positivists [maintain] that the only valid accounts are those graced with objective, methodologically correct procedures. [This stance] is at best false advertising and self-interested. It denies the complexities of social life . . . [and] lead[s] to distortion and oversimplification. . . .What is left is a move toward multiple methods and approaches" (Smith, 1994, pp. 42–43).

This chapter has endeavored to contribute to the movement toward mixed methods. Concentrating on the paradigmatic level of the debate, we first outlined three primary mixed-method stances on the sensibleness and defensibility of mixing paradigms while mixing methods. Then, in an effort to move the conversation beyond these stances, we analyzed two underlying issues. In terms of the relationship between inquiry paradigms and practice, we suggested that a reciprocal, mutually respectful, dialogic relationship between philosophical frameworks and methodological decisions is most warranted. Regarding the nature of paradigm attributes that matter most in mixed-method contexts, we focused on moving beyond the dead-end preoccupation with age-worn, irreconcilable paradigm attributes (such as objectivity versus subjectivity) to a new analytic space. This new space can encourage creative and imaginative mixed-method conversations, filled with multiple ways of knowing and acting—conversations that are generative and transformative in their potential insights and import. In this troubled era, with social problems of ever-increasing complexity and intractability, multiple ways of knowing and acting are surely needed.

## References

Bednarz, D. "Quantity and Quality in Evaluation Research: A Divergent View." *Evaluation and Program Planning,* 1985, *8,* 289–306.

Bernstein, R. J. *The New Constellation: The Ethical-Political Horizons of Modernity/Postmodernity.* Cambridge, England: Polity Press, 1993.

Brewer, J., and Hunter, A. *Multimethod Research: A Synthesis of Styles.* Thousand Oaks, Calif.: Sage, 1989.

Bryman, A. *Quantity and Quality in Social Research.* London: Unwin Hyman, 1988.

Campbell, D. T. "Reforms as Experiments." *American Psychologist,* 1969, *24,* 409–429.

Campbell, D. T. "Coherentist Empiricism, Hermeneutics, and the Commensurability of Paradigms." *International Journal of Educational Research,* 1991, *15,* 587–597.

Campbell, D. T., and Fiske, D. W. "Convergent and Discriminant Validation by the Multitrait-Multimethod Matrix." *Psychological Bulletin,* 1959, *56,* 81–105.

Caracelli, V. J., and Greene, J. C. "Data Analysis Strategies for Mixed-Method Evaluation Designs." *Educational Evaluation and Policy Analysis,* 1993, *15* (2), 195–207.

Cherryholmes, C. H. *Power and Criticism: Poststructural Investigations in Education.* New York: Teachers College Press, 1988.

Cook, T. D. "Postpositivist Critical Multiplism." In R. L. Shotland and M. M. Mark (eds.), *Social Science and Social Policy.* Thousand Oaks, Calif.: Sage, 1985.

Creswell, J. W. *Research Design: Qualitative and Quantitative Approaches.* Thousand Oaks, Calif.: Sage, 1994.

Denzin, N. K. "Triangulation." In D. K. Denzin (ed.), *The Research Act: An Introduction to Sociological Methods.* New York: McGraw-Hill, 1978.

Fielding, N. G., and Fielding, J. L. *Linking Data.* Qualitative Research Methods Series, no. 4. Thousand Oaks, Calif.: Sage, 1986.

Firestone, W. A. "Accommodation: Toward a Paradigm-Praxis Dialectic." In E. G. Guba (ed.), *The Paradigm Dialog.* Thousand Oaks, Calif.: Sage, 1990.

Fishman, D. B. (ed.). "Epistemological Paradigms for Evaluation, Special Issue." *Evaluation and Program Planning,* 1991, *14,* 351–410.

Geertz, C. "From the Native's Point of View: On the Nature of Anthropological Understanding." In P. Rabinow and W. Sullivan (eds.), *Interpretive Social Science.* Berkeley: University of California Press, 1979.

Giddens, G. *New Rules of Sociological Method.* New York: Basic Books, 1976.

Greene, J. C., Caracelli, V. J., and Graham, W. F. "Toward a Conceptual Framework Mixed-Method Evaluation Design." *Educational Evaluation and Policy Analysis,* 1989, *11,* 255–274.

Guba, E. G., and Lincoln, Y. S. *Fourth Generation Evaluation.* Thousand Oaks, Calif.: Sage, 1989.

House, E. R. "Integrating the Quantitative and the Qualitative." In C. S. Reichardt and S. F. Rallis (eds.), *The Qualitative-Quantitative Debate: New Perspectives.* New Directions for Program Evaluation, no. 61. San Francisco: Jossey-Bass, 1994.

Howe, K. R. "Two Dogmas of Educational Research." *Educational Researcher,* 1985, *14* (8), 10–18.

Howe, K. R. "Against the Quantitative-Qualitative Incompatibility Thesis, or Dogmas Die Hard." *Educational Researcher,* 1988, *17* (8), 10–16.

Howe, K. R., and Eisenhart, M. "Standards for Qualitative and Quantitative Research: A Prolegomenon." *Educational Researcher,* 1990, *19* (4), 2–9.

Kessels, J. P., and Korthagen, F. A. "The Relationship Between Theory and Practice: Back to the Classics." *Educational Researcher,* 1996, *25* (3), 17–22.

Kidder, L. H., and Fine, M. "Qualitative and Quantitative Methods: When Stories Converge." In M. M. Mark and R. L. Shotland (eds.), *Multiple Methods in Program Evaluation.* New Directions for Program Evaluation, no. 35. San Francisco: Jossey-Bass, 1987.

Krantz, D. L. "Sustaining Versus Resolving the Quantitative-Qualitative Debate." *Evaluation and Program Planning,* 1995, *18,* 89–96.

Lincoln, Y. S. "The Arts and Sciences of Program Evaluation." *Evaluation Practice,* 1991, *12* (1), 1–7.

Lincoln, Y. S., and Guba, E. G. *Naturalistic Inquiry.* Thousand Oaks, Calif.: Sage, 1985.

Mark, M. M., and Shotland, R. L. (eds.). *Multiple Methods in Program Evaluation.* New Directions for Program Evaluation, no. 35. San Francisco: Jossey-Bass, 1987.

Maxwell, J. A. *Qualitative Research Design: An Interactive Approach.* Applied Social Research Methods Series, no. 41. Thousand Oaks, Calif.: Sage, 1996.

Patton, M. Q. "Paradigms and Pragmatism." In D. M. Fetterman (ed.), *Qualitative Approaches to Evaluation in Education: The Silent Scientific Revolution.* New York: Praeger, 1988.

Patton, M. Q. *Qualitative Evaluation and Research Methods.* (2nd ed.) Thousand Oaks, Calif.: Sage, 1990.

Phelan, P. "Compatibility of Qualitative and Quantitative Methods: Studying Child Sexual Abuse in America." *Education and Urban Society,* 1987, *20* (1), 35–41.

Ragin, C. C. *The Comparative Method: Moving Beyond Qualitative and Quantitative Strategies.* Berkeley: University of California Press, 1989.

Reichardt, C. S., and Cook, T. D. "Beyond Qualitative *Versus* Quantitative Methods." In T. D. Cook and C. S. Reichardt (eds.), *Qualitative and Quantitative Methods in Evaluation Research.* Thousand Oaks, Calif.: Sage, 1979.

Reichardt, C. S., and Rallis, S. F. (eds.). *The Qualitative-Quantitative Debate: New Perspectives.* New Directions for Program Evaluation, no. 61. San Francisco: Jossey-Bass, 1994.

Riggin, L.J.C., and Caracelli, V. J. "Mixed-Method Evaluation: Developing Quality Criteria Through Concept Mapping." *Evaluation Practice,* 1994, *15* (2), 139–152.

Rossman, G. B., and Wilson, B. L. "Numbers and Words: Combining Quantitative and Qualitative Methods in a Single Large-Scale Evaluation Study." *Evaluation Review,* 1985, *9,* 627–643.

Rowles, G. D., and Reinharz, S. "Qualitative Gerontology: Themes and Challenges." In S. Reinharz and G. D. Rowles (eds.), *Qualitative Gerontology*. New York: Springer, 1987.

Salomon, G. "Transcending the Qualitative-Quantitative Debate: The Analytic and Systemic Approaches to Educational Research." *Educational Researcher,* 1991, *20* (6), 10–18.

Schwandt, T. A. "The Landscape of Value in Evaluation: Charted Terrain and Unexplored Territory." Paper presented at the annual meeting of the American Evaluation Association, Atlanta, 1996.

Sechrest, L. "Roots: Back to Our First Generations." *Evaluation Practice,* 1992, *13* (1), 1–7.

Shadish, W. R. (ed.). "The Quantitative-Qualitative Debates: 'DeKuhnifying' the Conceptual Context." *Evaluation and Program Planning,* 1995, *18*, 47–49.

Shotland, R. L., and Mark, M. M. "Improving Inferences from Multiple Methods." In M. M. Mark and R. L. Shotland (eds.), *Multiple Methods in Program Evaluation.* New Directions for Program Evaluation, no. 35. San Francisco: Jossey-Bass, 1987.

Smith, J. K. "Quantitative Versus Qualitative: An Attempt to Clarify the Issue." *Educational Researcher,* 1983, *12,* 6–13.

Smith, J. K. *The Nature of Social and Educational Inquiry: Empiricism Versus Interpretivism.* Norwood, N.J.: Ablex, 1989.

Smith, M. L. "Qualitative Plus/Versus Quantitative: The Last Word." In C. S. Reichardt and S. F. Rallis (eds.), *The Qualitative-Quantitative Debate: New Perspectives.* New Directions for Program Evaluation, no. 61. San Francisco: Jossey-Bass, 1994.

Willenbring, M. L., and Spicer, P. G. "Symmetry and Complementarity in Qualitative and Quantitative Evaluation Strategies." Paper presented at the annual meeting of the American Evaluation Association, New Orleans, 1991.

*JENNIFER C. GREENE is associate professor of human service studies at Cornell University. Her evaluation work concentrates on qualitative, participatory, and mixed-method approaches.*

*VALERIE J. CARACELLI is senior social science analyst at the U.S. General Accounting Office.*

*Two classes of mixed-method, mixed-paradigm evaluation designs are defined and described.*

# Crafting Mixed-Method Evaluation Designs

*Valerie J. Caracelli, Jennifer C. Greene*

The field of evaluation has shifted away from parochial debates and toward more ecumenical perspectives that seriously consider the potential of multiple, diverse inquiry methodologies to inform the purpose and practice of evaluative inquiry. Chelimsky (1997) identifies a superordinate goal for evaluation as it moves into the next century and into a more global context: the worldwide evaluation community must help respond to the urgent socioeconomic, political, and infrastructure needs that changing political and policy contexts have newly created. Chelimsky argues that part of our response must involve confronting two long-standing tensions in the evaluation field. The first concerns the different purposes for evaluation and the different methodological emphases they imply; the second concerns different views about the use of evaluation and different conceptions of the evaluator's role. To address our methodological problems, Chelimsky recommends an extended vision of evaluation, more skepticism about our methods, and the initiation of a "constructive dialogue in which we seek to correct weaknesses, not exacerbate them" (p. 23).

Chapter One of this volume builds on a broad, ecumenical view of methods to initiate what we hope will be a "constructive dialog" about the nature and influence of paradigms in framing mixed-method approaches to evaluation. The key tenet advanced is the need to move beyond debating paradigmatic differences that may well be irreconcilable and to focus instead on joining the critical features of our evaluative claims that represent distinct traditions. Joining such critical features can help to generate more relevant, useful, and discerning inferences. In this chapter, we relate the conceptual ideas advanced in Chapter One to several practical mixed-method design alternatives, accompanied by examples.

## Method Choices in Context: Some Caveats

Before we proceed, several considerations merit attention. First, our efforts to articulate mixed-paradigm design alternatives derive from our reading of both theoretical and empirical literature and our in-depth analysis of selected examples. Yet, evaluators rarely present their work with an explicit statement of the philosophical or value frameworks that guided their evaluation. When inquirers omit such information, we must infer whether quantitative and qualitative methods were used within a single paradigm or multiple paradigms. Guided by disciplinary conventions and critical features of the context, we have assumed, for example, that a randomized experiment that includes an ethnographic component constitutes a mixed-paradigm design. But even this assumption is challenged by the different inquiry traditions in specific disciplines. Ethnography, for example, has been linked to three different paradigms in anthropology, ranging from phenomenological to more behaviorist modes of inquiry (Firestone, 1987).

Second, discrete classification of methods as qualitative or quantitative is not always straightforward (Hedrick, 1994; Langenbach, Vaughn, and Aagaard, 1994). A survey is usually thought to represent a quantitative methodology. Yet, surveys generally begin with some qualitative base to ensure context-relevant interpretation of questions and may include open-ended responses, resulting in an instrument with mixed-method characteristics. (See Suchman and Jordan, 1990, for seminal advances in qualitative aspects of survey methodology.) Moreover, our conventional notions of surveys are challenged in cross-cultural research, in which surveys of rural communities may rely on participatory and interactive techniques that include maps and pictures depicting the phenomena of interest (Buenavista and Flora, 1994; Lightfoot, Feldman, and Abedin, 1994). Similarly, case studies frequently associated with qualitative methodology can include a combination of methods and can be carried out within a critical realist framework (Yin, 1989) or an interpretivist one (Stake, 1994).

Third, we recognize that although many evaluation practitioners care about method choices, they care more intensely about responding responsibly to the very important questions that arise in the development and evaluation of social programs. Different questions reflect different evaluation purposes—accountability, organizational learning, social reform—and, in turn, the questions influence evaluators' differential selection of methods (Chelimsky, 1997; Patton, 1997). In short, we acknowledge that method choices are not as neatly demarcated nor as politically unfettered as the present discussion suggests.

## Combining Critical Features of Inquiry Paradigms: Extant Ideas

Pragmatic advice in designing evaluations under the umbrella of multimethod research (Brewer and Hunter, 1989; Mark and Shotland, 1987), and more specifically with regard to combining qualitative and quantitative methods

(Cook and Reichardt, 1979; Creswell, 1994; Fielding and Fielding, 1986; Reichardt and Rallis, 1994), has become a part of methodological guidance for the practitioner.

Creswell (1994) offers several models for combined methods designs. These models, however, align quantitative methods with a quantitative paradigm and qualitative methods with a qualitative paradigm. This obscures how both method types can be used within a single inquiry framework to construct knowledge. This alignment also makes it difficult to discern when recommended design strategies are actually combining features of different paradigmatic traditions.

Langenbach, Vaughn, and Aagaard (1994) attend to the intersections of three inquiry dimensions: (1) ontology, or the degree to which an inquiry represents perspective-seeking or truth-seeking philosophical traditions; (2) epistemology, represented by contrasting quantitative and qualitative methodologies; and (3) ideology, or the social, moral, or political stances that influence studies toward reform or toward retaining the status quo. This model is useful for describing the complexity of method selection within a single paradigm. For example, the authors view understanding perspectives as a critical feature of interpretivist modes of inquiry and the ability to generalize from findings as a critical feature of truth-seeking, postempiricist modes of inquiry. Studies within these frameworks can vary in the degree to which they rely on quantitative or qualitative methods, alone or in combination, and in the degree to which conservative or reformist ideologies permeate the research. Langenbach, Vaughn, and Aagaard, however, stop short of describing how these critical features can be combined in a single study. They also do not consider combining other critical features associated with these traditions, such as those outlined in Chapter One.

Julnes (1995) takes the concept of combining critical features of different inquiry frameworks and moves it forward. He charts out how multiple methods within a critical realist perspective can integrate two important inquiry dimensions: deduction versus induction, and molar versus molecular causality. He discusses these dimensions, typically associated with validation and interpretivist frameworks, respectively, in terms of their potential for strengthening theory-guided practice and study conclusions.

Julnes illustrates the advantages for *both* interpretivist and quantitative methodologies of an iterative process that moves between induction and deduction for explanatory purposes. He argues that the benefits of this iterative process, when used with qualitative approaches, are equally applicable to quantitative methodologies. Julnes also argues for integrating two views of causality (molar and molecular), associated with different inquiry traditions, to strengthen causal conclusions and enrich descriptions of phenomena. The molar causal impact of the program (the probabilistic net effect of multiple causes) is understood as comprising molecular activities that, when analyzed as links between particular antecedents and particular consequences, can delineate mediating and moderating relationships. Thus, theory can become more precise and conclusions strengthened through the richer pattern of outcomes obtained when these distinct views of causality are combined.

Julnes's work offers a fine illustration of the potential power of combining critical features of knowledge claims representing different paradigmatic traditions. He presents these knowledge claims as potentially being mutually informative rather than inherently conflictual. When combined in a mixed-method study, they have the ability to provide significantly more germane and useful information than would be obtained if, as in Julnes's example, only structural explanations were sought without contextual understanding. The design alternatives presented next provide a framework within which these conceptual ideas about mixing critical features of evaluative claims can be explored practically.

## Linking Paradigms Through Design Options

Defensible and coherent mixed-method design options appear to cluster within two broad classes: component designs and integrated designs. Although the designs featured within these broad classifications share the aim of generating more comprehensive and insightful understanding of phenomena, they can be distinguished by the level of methods integration designed and achieved in the evaluative inquiry.

**Mixed-Method Component Designs.** In component designs, the methods are implemented as discrete aspects of the overall inquiry and remain distinct throughout the inquiry. The combining of different method components occurs at the level of interpretation and conclusion rather than at prior stages of data collection or analysis. In contrast to integrated designs, component designs do not readily lend themselves to generating dialectically transformed understandings and insights. This can occur, however, especially in instances of nonconvergence or when theoretical expectations meet with anomalous information. Alternatively, as Mark, Feller, and Button point out in Chapter Four of this volume, when inquirer expectancies encounter discrepant information, the problem may be methods-based and the solution might involve assessing and correcting for bias. Three specific component designs—triangulation, complementarity, and expansion—build directly on our earlier work, which identified specific purposes for mixing methods (Greene, Caracelli, and Graham, 1989).

A rich literature already surrounds the implementation of *triangulation designs* in which different methods are used to assess the same phenomenon toward convergence and increased validity. Related to triangulation, the bracketing design (Mark and Shotland, 1987; Reichardt and Gollob, 1987) seeks a range of estimates using methods biased in opposite directions. Across studies, the postpositivist cross-design synthesis strategy (which relies on triangulation and bracketing logic) builds on existing meta-analytic techniques for combining quantitative outcomes across a set of studies (Droitcour, in press; Droitcour, Silberman, and Chelimsky, 1993). The hallmark of this approach is its focus on combining results from studies with complementary designs to minimize study biases that derive from inherent design weaknesses (for example, randomized controlled trials that are limited in external validity are combined with database analyses that can be generalized to a broader population but are problematic with regard to selection bias). The cross-design synthesis strategy requires assessing study bias, adjusting for it, and synthesizing the study's adjusted results within and across design categories. The cross-design synthesis logic and strategy could be extended to combining different forms of coordinated data (qualitative and quantitative) about the same phenomena—data which were generated from disparate inquiry designs and frameworks. This expanded form of bracketing would encompass a broader range of sources of bias and design limitations, and, by offsetting such design weaknesses, it could have the potential to yield particularly strong and defensible inferences.

With *complementarity designs,* in which results from one dominant method type are enhanced or clarified by results from another method type, an extension can be readily made from the method to the paradigm level. Using interpretivist interviews that aim for depth and contextual relevance to supplement postpositivist surveys conducted for breadth and representativeness might be considered a classic complementarity component design.

*Expansion designs* can also be readily extended to the paradigm level. In these designs, inquiry paradigms frame different methods that are used for distinct inquiry components—for example, implementation and outcome assessment. The results are characteristically offered in a side-by-side fashion, as illustrated by the Willenbring and Spicer example in Chapter One.

**Mixed-Method Integrated Designs.** In contrast to component designs, this class of design characteristically attains a greater integration of the different method types. The methods can be mixed in ways that integrate elements of disparate paradigms and have the potential to produce significantly more insightful, even dialectically transformed, understandings of the phenomenon under investigation. In this class of design, we discuss four basic types: (1) iterative, (2) embedded or nested, (3) holistic, and (4) transformative. In the fourth type of integrated design, the valuing of paradigmatic coherence, which is characteristic of the first three types, is replaced by a valuing of pluralistic values and action. Although these designs do not exhaust the potential variations of mixed-method integrated models, they serve to illustrate that critical features of knowledge claims from different inquiry frameworks can be combined in an evaluation meaningfully and successfully. A brief explication of these four integrated designs is followed by illustrative examples.

*Iterative designs* are characterized by a dynamic and ongoing interplay over time between the different methodologies associated with different paradigms. Studies engaging in a single iteration can serve the mixed-method purpose of development in which the results from one method type are used to inform the development of the other method type. With multiple iterations, the study enables a progressive reconfiguration of substantive findings and interpretations in a pattern of increasing insight and sophistication. This spiral type of design is exemplified by Phelan's study of incest (1987), described in Chapter One. Phelan's progressively sophisticated insights integrated the interpretivist's focus on the emic meaning of sexual behavior with the survey methodologist's attention to families' structural characteristics.

*Embedded or nested designs* feature one methodology located within another, interlocking contrasting inquiry characteristics in a framework of creative tension. Jacob's study (1982) conducted in Puerto Rico on the influences of culture and environment on children's cognition demonstrates how the integral joining of ethnography and path analysis can yield a depth and breadth of information not possible if only one approach has been selected. The data resulting from dovetailing these methodologies convey both the meaning of naturally occurring behaviors in their social contexts and the frequencies representing macrolevel relationships. Jacob discusses how interpretations and conclusions from combining different paradigmatic features during all stages of inquiry can be of great value to researchers, practitioners, and policymakers alike.

*Holistic designs* highlight the necessary interdependence of different methodologies for understanding complex phenomena fully. There is a simultaneity of the integration of methods in these designs rather than a sense of taking turns. This genre of design may take the form of a conceptual framework that guides the design and implementation of the whole study. For example, articulating a program theory (Chen, 1989) or using concept-mapping techniques (Maxwell, 1996; Trochim, 1989) at the outset of a study can provide a substantive framework for integrating disparate methods, meanings, and understandings. An integrated synthesis of methodologies can also occur at the analysis stage. To illustrate, Ragin's synthesis (1989) of case-oriented and variable-oriented inquiry approaches is intended to address more than a handful of cases while retaining the complex, conjoined, causal explanations of those cases. The intention is to be sensitive to human agency and social processes, as well as to structural processes. The approach is holistic, so the cases themselves are not lost, and the approach is analytic, so some generalization is possible. Integration is also an attribute of Scriven's proposals (1995) for aggregating disparate evaluative results into one overall judgment. Additionally, in Chapter Six of this volume, see Smith's innovative extension of Erickson's integrative analytic method (1986) in a mixed-method context.

*Transformative designs* are distinctive because they give primacy to the value-based and action-oriented dimensions of different inquiry traditions. The emphasis is on mixing the value commitments of different traditions for better representation of multiple interests and the value pluralism of the larger social context. Such designs are transformative in that they offer opportunities for reconfiguring the dialog across ideological differences and, thus, have the potential to restructure the evaluation context. In this type of design, diverse methods most importantly serve to include a broader set of interests in the resulting knowledge claims and to strengthen the likely effectiveness of action solutions. This type of design appears most frequently in evaluative inquiry featuring participatory, action-research, empowerment approaches (Everitt, 1996; Reiben, 1996).

We will now illustrate several of the integrated designs, emphasizing the manner in which specific features of different inquiry frameworks were combined. We focus on these designs both because they have received less attention in the literature than component designs and because the substantive and methodological integration they are capable of achieving warrants further exploration.

## Integrated Design Options in Evaluation Practice

As noted, *iterative* designs are characterized by a time sequence in which study results achieve a greater depth and richness through successive iterations of the study and reformulations of study findings. Eckert visually depicts this design as a spiral in his multistage project entitled "Unseen Community: Old Nonwelfare Poor in Urban Hotels" (1987). In this eight-year study of older hotel dwellers living in an urban area undergoing revitalization and development, Eckert demonstrates how he used components of different inquiry frameworks to preserve "the insights and understanding derived from qualitative/experiential approaches while enhancing the ability to replicate, verify, and generalize findings" (p. 242).

The research proceeded in three stages. The first stage began with a general question about how older hotel dwellers survive in a changing urban environment. A key component of this ethnographic phase was conceptualizing what "community" meant, with the understanding that both "outsider" (etic) and "insider" (emic) perspectives were important to capture. For example, the older hotel dwellers regarded downtown as "home" and the several blocks around their hotels as providing them with an infrastructure critical to survival, including local restaurants, supportive services, and opportunities for activities. From the outsider perspective, city planners, the media, and the general public perceived the area as a "skid row" or "tenderloin" district with substandard "greasy spoon" restaurants. The study did not differentiate older hotel dwellers from drifters, winos, and vagrants. The solution to what was considered an urban blight problem, from this etic perspective, was to target a sixteen-block area for redevelopment and investment, moving undesirables out to less visible areas of town.

The second and third stages of this spiral study examined the short- and long-term effects of involuntary relocation on the older people's health, social networks, activity patterns, and psychosocial adjustment. In these stages, Eckert used a quasi-experimental design to test relevant propositions that emerged from the initial ethnography. Contrary to expectations, there were no significant changes in physical, functional, or emotional health for those forced to relocate and those in a matched comparison group. Eckert believes that because the in-depth longitudinal study helped him understand certain factors—such as the process of relocation, the nature of environmental change, the social services available, and the personal characteristics of the hotel dwellers—he could better interpret the quantitative findings.

Eckert notes that "stages 1 through 3 were tightly intertwined, feeding back information and insight into one another. Initial inductive and idiographic strategies melded into increasingly deductive and nomothetic strategies. The observational and qualitative data informed and guided the efforts to quantify and test given hypotheses" (p. 254). Eckert characterized several aspects of the design as contributing to the quality of the study. Including both emic and etic perspectives—critical features associated with contrasting paradigms—reduced the likelihood of erroneous assumptions and conclusions from an a priori adoption of an etic perspective. Emic concepts and categories increased the validity of the research questions and enhanced the operationalization of concepts during later, more deductive stages of the investigation. Furthermore, inductive and deductive tensions viewed as incommensurable within a single study were accommodated in the longitudinal aspects of this spiral design, as earlier study findings enabled the formulation of new and important questions about the survival of elderly, nonwelfare, poor persons in a changing urban environment.

A second integrated design is the *embedded* or *nested* design, in which the study is framed by one methodology within which a different methodology is located. In Maxwell, Bashook, and Sandlow (1986), ethnographic methods were used within an experimental framework in order to evaluate the educational value of physicians' participation in one hospital's medical care evaluation (MCE) committees. These committees were responsible for regularly reviewing patient records against explicit criteria for the treatment of particular disorders. The committees aimed to identify patterns or instances in which the quality of care could be improved. The study began with an ethnographic investigation of existing MCEs, and used participant observation to identify factors that contributed to the committees' educational value. Ethnographic portrayals of each committee were developed and analyzed for differences between committees identified as having high and low educational value.

An experimental program was then developed to increase the educational value of the MCEs. Ethnographic investigation continued in order to assess the program's impact on committees' functioning and learning. Transcripts of committee meetings were analyzed for learning opportunities, which were later corroborated through peer debriefings. Multiple measures, including knowledge tests, clinical case recall interviews, and a review of patient records, were used to assess knowledge and performance outcomes. Questionnaires were used to determine physicians' attitudes. The conclusion that MCEs had a causal role in changing knowledge and performance was strengthened by a series of contrasts that showed that the knowledge gains did not occur in matched control groups, or for control topics in the knowledge tests, but did take place in successful committees. The authors believed that, on the one hand, the experimental controls reduced bias "without sacrificing the richness of data and access to participants' meanings provided by the ethnographic methods" (Maxwell, Bashook, and Sandlow, 1986, p. 139).

On the other hand, the ethnographic investigation was able to illuminate the causal processes operating in the setting—processes which increased the interpretability of the experimental outcomes.

The study was intentionally designed with paradigmatic criteria in mind in order to join the critical features of meaning and understanding with causal explanation. The authors concluded that the ethnographic component allowed them to discover unanticipated aspects of the educational processes that occur in the MCEs, aspects they would have missed if they had relied entirely on quantitative methods. The warrant for these ethnographic insights was substantially strengthened by the experimental controls. A key part of this study was recasting how MCEs influenced physicians' performance. An assumption in the design of the experiment was that participation in the committees would directly increase the physicians' knowledge. Instead, the ethnographic data revealed that the program's effects were achieved indirectly by increasing the physicians' confidence in applying knowledge that they already possessed.

*Holistic* designs constitute a varied set of promising mixed-method models. In these designs, the mixed-method tension invoked by juxtaposing different inquiry facets is transferred to a substantive framework, which then becomes the structure within which integration occurs. For example, in Chen's approach (1990) to theory-based evaluation, program theory is the critical substantive framework for mixing methods. In Chapter Five of this volume, Chen illustrates how, under particular circumstances, one can enhance a program theory framework by including mixed methods. It is especially notable when critical features of paradigms, such as "depth" of information (particularity, closeness, contextualized understanding of local meanings) and "width" of information (generality, distance, analysis of regularities), are both needed if a theoretical understanding of substantive dimensions and issues pertaining to the program is to be explicated better.

Another example of an integrative substantive framework relevant to mixed methods is a concept map—for instance, the spatial map yielded by Trochim's structured conceptualization process (1989). An illustrative study using this concept-mapping process was developing a mission statement and future plan for the community service commitment of a local Catholic church (Trochim and others, 1991). This project included four substudies; the first relied on concept mapping. Input to the concept mapping process comprised community service issues raised across a broad spectrum of parishioners and other interest groups. The parish council consolidated these issues into ninety-seven statements and then sorted and rated them. Multidimensional scaling and cluster analyses of these sort-and-rate data then yielded a concept map, which offered a visual representation of how this parish envisioned its community service commitment.

Consisting of several conceptual clusters, this concept map also provided an organizing framework for the design and implementation of the other three substudies in this project, which involved a mixture of methods. In the second substudy, focus groups were conducted and oriented toward discussing some of the clusters, including development of lay ministry, family and youth spiritual enrichment, and spirituality. The third substudy used interviews with key respondents (staff, council members, parishioners, local community leaders, other faith groups, and nearby Catholic community leaders), exploring in greater detail issues identified in the focus groups. The fourth substudy extended data collection to all members of the parish through a mail survey that included two survey items from each of the clusters.

The concept map also provided the conceptual structure for data consolidation across the mixed-method substudies. While analyses were conducted separately for each substudy (or method), the clusters on the map provided the structure for integrating key findings and recommendations across substudies or methods. A unifying theme among study findings was the parishioners' desire for greater spirituality and sense of community. The integrative framework offered by the concept map in this study allowed for the representation of very divergent expressions of how a sense of spiritual community could be achieved, ranging from more emphasis on traditional ceremony to greater efforts in ministering to those in need. The authors noted that "these differences provide the basis for some tension in the parish community especially when we forget that they represent different paths to the very commonly held ideal of community spirituality" (Trochim and others, 1991, p. 24). Study conclusions speak to the necessity of a mission statement and pastoral plan that can accommodate the great diversity in the parish as it moves toward that broad consensual goal.

An emphasis on program theory or a focus on representing the conceptual domain of an evaluation through a stakeholder-based process such as concept mapping can serve as a structure for integrating diverse methods and knowledge claims. In Chapter Six of this volume, Smith posits that mental models, carried by inquirers and representing their assumptions and proclivities about how knowledge is constructed, also serve as integrative structures for deriving coherent knowledge claims from a diverse set of methodologies. Examples of holistically integrated designs also include the data consolidation method developed by Louis (1981), Ragin's synthesis of case-oriented and variable-oriented strategies (1989), and undoubtedly other creative variations.

In an example of *transformative* design, Greene and others (n.d.) evaluated the first year of Grandview High School's new science program. This program emphasized students' active construction, rather than passive acquisition, of knowledge. Program goals included fostering scientific literacy and developing scientific reasoning, and program activities emphasized hands-on work with content relevant to students' lives. The program also included "detracking," which involved merging the high school's two college-bound tracks into one. The Grandview community widely accepted the pedagogical changes in this program. Detracking, however, met with considerable controversy. A vocal group of opponents to the change were concerned that their children would not be adequately challenged in the merged classes, nor competitively prepared for admission to exclusive colleges and universities. Another group of vocal supporters was committed to upgrading the educational opportunities for poor children and children of color in the school system. This group viewed detracking as an essential reform.

The members of the evaluation team intentionally adopted a *critical educative* evaluation stance in their role as evaluators. The intention, realized through a mixed-method framework relying on different inquiry traditions, was to give voice to the many diverse program positions and value stances that accompanied this reform. More important, the evaluation focus was to promote and encourage dialog and deliberation. Methodologically, the aims were implemented through sampling strategies that maximized heterogeneity, and through interview guides and questionnaires that sought perceptions on a wide range of dimensions of this science reform. In this design, the rationale for mixing methods had less to do with methodology and more to do with values or ideology. The reliance on mixed methods in this evaluation was primarily to represent pluralistic interests, voices, and perspectives better and, through this representation, both to challenge and transform entrenched positions through the dialog that the evaluation inquiry fostered.

## Epilogue

As part of Chelimsky's superordinate goal that we quoted at the outset of this chapter, we intended to initiate a "constructive dialog" about the role of paradigms in mixed-method evaluative inquiry. Building on the conceptual ideas advanced in Chapter One, this chapter discussed mixed-method design alternatives that have the potential to combine critical features of paradigmatic traditions defensibly and coherently. As argued in Chapter One, these different facets of knowledge claims are neither differentially valuable nor inherently incompatible in logic.

This chapter offered two broad classes of mixed-method designs that can include elements of different paradigms: component designs and integrated designs. These design classes are distinguished by the degree, nature, and timing of the mix of methods and their critical features. In component designs, the mix is conducted at the end stages of inquiry; in integrated designs, the mix is conducted at multiple stages of inquiry for purposes of reframing questions, reconstructing instruments, reanalyzing data, or refining interpretations and conclusions.

Although the chapter emphasized integrated mixed-method designs because they have received less attention in the literature, both classes of design are important in evaluation practice. We believe that mixed-method component designs are more likely to be implemented when pragmatic considerations hold sway. Mixed-method integrated designs may be more likely to offer dialectical potential. But these are descriptive linkages, not limiting prescriptions. More important is the common emphasis in both classes of design on joining identifiable critical features of the inquiry traditions that are being mixed. The resulting knowledge claims are enriched precisely because they incorporate and honor diverse critical features, rather than relying on a relatively restricted and homogeneous set.

The careful planning and considered judgments these designs require should contribute to a repertoire of sound mixed-method inquiry approaches that can help improve evaluation practice. In the chapters that follow, these conceptual and practical ideas about mixing methods will be explored and expanded further.

## References

Brewer, J., and Hunter, A. *Multimethod Research: A Synthesis of Styles.* Thousand Oaks, Calif.: Sage, 1989.

Buenavista, G., and Flora, C. B. "Participatory Methodologies for Analyzing Household Activities, Resources, and Benefits." In H. S. Feldstein and J. Jiggins (eds.), *Tools for the Field: Methodologies Handbook for Gender Analysis in Agriculture.* West Hartford, Conn.: Kumarian Press, 1994.

Chelimsky, E. "The Coming Transformations in Evaluation." In E. Chelimsky and W. R. Shadish (eds.), *Evaluation for the Twenty-First Century.* Thousand Oaks, Calif.: Sage, 1997.

Chen, H.-T. "The Conceptual Framework of the Theory-Driven Perspective." *Evaluation and Program Planning,* 1989, *12,* 391–396.

Chen, H.-T. "Issues in Constructing Program Theory." In L. Bickman (ed.), *Advances in Program Theory.* New Directions for Program Evaluation, no. 47. San Francisco: Jossey-Bass, 1990.

Cook, T. D., and Reichardt, C. S. (eds.). *Qualitative and Quantitative Methods in Evaluation Research.* Thousand Oaks, Calif.: Sage, 1979.

Creswell, J. W. *Research Design: Qualitative and Quantitative Approaches.* Thousand Oaks, Calif.: Sage, 1994.

Droitcour, J. "Cross-Design Synthesis: Concept and Application." In E. Chelimsky and W. R. Shadish (eds.), *Evaluation for the Twenty-First Century.* Thousand Oaks, Calif.: Sage, in press.

Droitcour, J., Silberman, G., and Chelimsky, E. "Cross-Design Synthesis: A New Form of Meta-Analysis for Combining Results from Randomized Clinical Trials and Medical-Practice Databases." *International Journal of Technology Assessment in Health Care,* 1993, *9* (3), 440–449.

Eckert, J. K. "Ethnographic Research on Aging." In S. Reinharz and G. D. Rowles (eds.), *Qualitative Gerontology.* New York: Springer, 1987.

Erickson, F. E. "Qualitative Methods in Research on Teaching." In M. Wittrock (ed.), *Handbook of Research on Teaching.* (3rd ed.) Old Tappan, N.J.: Macmillan, 1986.

Everitt, A. "Developing Critical Evaluation." *Evaluation,* 1996, *2,* 173–188.

Fielding, N. G., and Fielding, J. L. *Linking Data.* Qualitative Research Methods Series, no. 4. Thousand Oaks, Calif.: Sage, 1986.

Firestone, W. A. "Meaning in Method: The Rhetoric of Quantitative and Qualitative Research." *Educational Researcher,* 1987, *16* (7), 16–21.

Greene, J. C., Caracelli, V. J., and Graham, W. F. "Toward a Conceptual Framework for Mixed-Method Evaluation Designs." *Educational Evaluation and Policy Analysis,* 1989, *11* (3), 255–274.

Greene, J. C., Bowen, K., Cassaro, D., Cole, R., Galin, M., Goodyear, L. Grigoriu, E., Ingoglia, J., Jantzi, T., LaChance, A., and Shannon, C. "Final Evaluation Report, 'Grandview' High School Science Program, Year 1." Prepared for the 'Grandview' High School Science Evaluation Planning Committee, Ithaca, N.Y., n.d..

Hedrick, T. E. "The Quantitative-Qualitative Debate: Possibilities for Integration." In C. S. Reichardt and S. F. Rallis (eds.), *The Qualitative-Quantitative Debate: New Perspectives.* New Directions for Program Evaluation, no. 61. San Francisco: Jossey-Bass, 1994.

Jacob, E. "Combining Ethnographic and Quantitative Approaches: Suggestions and Examples from a Study on Puerto Rico." In P. Gilmore and A. A. Glatthorn (eds.), *Children in and out of School: Ethnography and Education.* Washington, D.C.: Center for Applied Linguistics, 1982.

Julnes, G. "Context-Confirmatory Methods for Supporting Disciplined Induction in Post-Positivist Inquiry." Paper presented at the annual meeting of the American Evaluation Association, Vancouver, Nov. 2, 1995.

Langenbach, M., Vaughn, C., and Aagaard, L. *An Introduction to Educational Research.* Boston: Allyn & Bacon, 1994.

Lightfoot, C., Feldman, S., and Abedin, M. Z. "Incorporating Gender in Conceptual Diagrams of Household and Agroecosystems." In H. S. Feldstein and J. Jiggins (eds.), *Tools for the Field: Methodologies Handbook for Gender Analysis in Agriculture.* West Hartford, Conn.: Kumarian Press, 1994.

Louis, K. S. "Policy Researcher as Sleuth: New Approaches to Integrating Qualitative and Quantitative Methods." Paper presented at the annual meeting of the American Educational Research Association, Los Angeles, Apr. 1981.

Mark, M. M., and Shotland, R. L. (eds.). *Multiple Methods in Program Evaluation.* New Directions for Program Evaluation, no. 35. San Francisco: Jossey-Bass, 1987.

Maxwell, J. A. "Conceptual Context: What Do You Think Is Going on?" In *Qualitative Research Design: An Interactive Approach.* Applied Social Research Methods Series, no. 41. Thousand Oaks, Calif.: Sage, 1996.

Maxwell, J. A., Bashook, P. G., and Sandlow, L. J. "Combining Ethnographic and Experimental Methods in Educational Evaluation: A Case Study." In D. Fetterman and M. A. Pitman (eds.), *Educational Evaluation: Ethnography in Theory, Practice, and Politics.* Thousand Oaks, Calif.: Sage, 1986.

Patton, M. Q. *Utilization-Focused Evaluation: The New Century Text.* Thousand Oaks, Calif.: Sage, 1997.

Phelan, P. "Compatibility of Qualitative and Quantitative Methods: Studying Child Sexual Abuse in America." *Education and Urban Society,* 1987, *20* (1), 35–41.

Ragin, C. C. *The Comparative Method: Moving Beyond Qualitative and Quantitative Strategies.* Berkeley: University of California Press, 1989.

Reiben, C. C. "Participatory Evaluation of Development Assistance: Dealing with Power and Facilitative Learning." *Evaluation,* 1996, *2,* 151–171.

Reichardt, C. S., and Gollob, H. F. "Taking Uncertainty into Account when Estimating Effects." In M. M. Mark and R. L. Shotland (eds.), *Multiple Methods in Program Evaluation.* New Directions for Program Evaluation, no. 35. San Francisco: Jossey-Bass, 1987.

Reichardt, C. S., and Rallis, S. F. (eds.). *The Qualitative-Quantitative Debate: New Perspectives.* New Directions for Program Evaluation, no. 61. San Francisco: Jossey-Bass, 1994.

Scriven, M. "The Logic of Evaluation and Evaluation Practice." In D. Fournier (ed.), *Reasoning in Evaluation: Inferential Links and Leaps.* New Directions for Evaluation, no. 68. San Francisco: Jossey-Bass, 1995.

Stake, R. E. "Case Studies." In N. K. Denzin and Y. S. Lincoln (eds.), *Handbook of Qualitative Research.* Thousand Oaks, Calif.: Sage, 1994.

Suchman, L., and Jordan, B. "Interactional Troubles in Face-to-Face Survey Interviews." *Journal of the American Statistical Association,* 1990, *85* (409), 232–253.

Trochim, W.M.K. (ed.). "Special Issue: Concept Mapping for Evaluation and Planning." *Evaluation and Program Planning,* 1989, *12* (1).

Trochim, W.M.K., Steidl, R., Hutchens, W., Wishart, J., Comas, C., Herbstman, W., Koen, J., Levine, B., and Tobias, M. "Final Report of the Data Gathering Committee." Unpublished paper, Cornell University, 1991.

Yin, R. K. *Case Study Research: Design and Methods.* Thousand Oaks, Calif.: Sage, 1989.

*Valerie J. Caracelli is senior social science analyst at the U.S. General Accounting Office.*

*Jennifer C. Greene is associate professor of human service studies at Cornell University. Her evaluation work concentrates on qualitative, participatory, and mixed-method approaches.*

*A pragmatic framework for making decisions about mixed-method
designs is proposed and then applied to illustrative evaluations to
help identify the strengths and limitations of making practical,
contextual, and consequential considerations a primary basis for
evaluation design decisions.*

# A Pragmatic Basis for
# Mixed-Method Designs

*Lois-ellin Datta*

*Once upon a time, in a country long, long ago, magistrates wanted to know whether
a new health program intended to lower costs was delivering quality care. The evaluators decided that existing measures and designs, such as facility inspection reports
and mortality rates, had deficiencies. The question, they concluded, could be
answered only after a comprehensive analysis had been made of what health care
quality was and how one could recognize it. Only this method would permit multiple, diverse perspectives. The magistrates asked how long this would take, sighed
deeply at the response, but approved the activity. The evaluators convened the wise
women and men of the country, no small undertaking in either logistics or prepara-
tion. They found themselves more perplexed than ever in the aftermath because the
wise men and women talked themselves into opposing and irreconcilable philosophical stances and hopelessly tangled analytic knots. The evaluators wrote up the con-
ference proceedings. However, the report was so long that even the participants used
it for a doorstop.*

*After some months of continuing to rely on facility inspection reports and mor-
tality rates, the magistrates turned to other evaluators. These evaluators took a more
pragmatic view. They examined the existing measures and designs and selected a sub-
set of measures (1) whose meaning was readily understandable, (2) in which the
weakness of one approach to data collection could be offset by the strengths of another,
and (3) for which information was fairly readily available about a sizable enough
group of health care recipients and providers under the new program and under the
old program. By and large, although each measure offered a different view of quality, findings generally converged. Before long, these evaluators completed a report.
They presented the strengths and limitations of each method and stated their findings
as ranges rather than as misleadingly precise averages. They told the magistrates*

New Directions for Evaluation, no. 74, Summer 1997 © Jossey-Bass Publishers

*that quality was lower under the new program, but not below a reasonable standard of adequacy. Costs had decreased, however, and more people were receiving service.*

This example and others like it raise questions about the benefits of a pragmatic approach to mixed-method designs, the price the position exacts in return for the benefits, and how some problems associated with this evaluative stance are solved. This chapter examines these questions first by defining a pragmatic basis for mixed-method design decisions, then by applying the framework derived from this basis to some illustrative evaluations, and finally by summarizing a few lessons learned about the pragmatic approach.

## A Pragmatic Basis Defined

"Pragmatic" is not a popular inclusion in indexes of some widely read sources for evaluation theory and definitions. It does not appear, for example, in *The Evaluation Thesaurus* (Scriven, 1990), *Evaluation Theory* (Chen, 1992), or *Guiding Principles for Evaluators* (Shadish, Newman, Scheirer, and Wye, 1995). It does, however, receive considerable attention in evaluation from authors such as Patton (1988, 1990), Skrtic (1990), and Schwandt (1990). Their discussions provide useful comments on the implications for the field of evaluation pragmatism as defined in its originating field by philosophers such as Dewey, Mead, Pierce, and more recent writers. The primary focus is on the results of the methods chosen, rather than, in Patton's words, "on the epistemology out of which they have emerged" (1990, p. 90). The qualities of the pragmatist's approach, as seen by various evaluators, include "a paradigm of choices," design flexibility, methodological appropriateness as the standard of quality, improved situational responsiveness, and a reliance on practical results and level of certainty as criteria of truth.

Drawing on these authors and the ideas of Greene (J. C. Greene, personal communication, 1996), I propose for our field that "pragmatic" mean *the essential criteria for making design decisions are practical, contextually responsive, and consequential.* "Practical" implies a basis in one's experience of what does and does not work. "Contextually responsive" involves understanding the demands, opportunities, and constraints of the situation in which the evaluation will take place. "Consequential" in this discussion is defined by pragmatic theory.

**Consequentiality and Pragmatic Theory.** Pragmatic theory, a well-developed area of philosophical inquiry, holds that the truth of a statement consists of its practical consequences, particularly the statement's agreement with subsequent experience. These practical consequences form standards by which concepts are analyzed and their validity determined. For the present discussion, a "statement" is taken to be "an evaluation design," which is arguably a statement about an acceptable way of carrying out an evaluation study.

This chapter considers how these three criteria—practicality, contextual responsiveness, and consequences—are applied to evaluation design, particularly mixed-method designs involving different kinds of methods. Following the approach of Greene and Caracelli (Chapter One of this volume), a mixed-method design intentionally combines quite different kinds of methods, such as qualitative and quantitative, variable-oriented and case-oriented, contemporaneous and historical. The combination may arise when different methods are applied to the same evaluation question or component, or when different methods are allocated to different evaluation questions (J. C. Greene, personal communication, 1996).

It should be noted that what constitutes a mixed method depends somewhat on the eye of the beholder. The U.S. General Accounting Office (1992), for example, discusses cross-design synthesis as combining data from randomized clinical trials and administrative databases.

What, then, should constitute a pragmatic framework for mixed-method evaluation design? *Guiding Principles for Evaluators* (Shadish, Newman, Scheirer, and Wye, 1995) offers many candidates for a pragmatic framework. Each principle has significant consequences for our field or for a specific evaluation. A closer look, however, reveals that most of the principles are not about methodological decisions. The pragmatic framework suggested below could be expanded to include questions from these guiding principles *as long as their practical consequences can be anticipated,* such as when context is taken into account or when the practical consequences can be shown in subsequent experience.

**A Pragmatic Framework.** Four questions about practical consequences of design decisions appear frequently in the evaluation literature. These are:

1. Can salient evaluation questions be adequately answered?
2. Can the design be successfully carried out, taking into consideration such issues as access to information, time available, evaluators' skills, and money or other resources required for the evaluation?
3. Are design trade-offs (for example, between depth of understanding and generalizability) optimized?
4. Are the results usable?

Each of these could unfold into subquestions. For example, considerations associated with "Can salient evaluation questions be adequately answered" include: (1) What is a salient evaluation question? (2) What makes for an adequate answer(s)? and (3) Whose standards of adequacy are important? For the purposes of the current analysis, however, the broad questions and their interplay take precedence in examining a pragmatic basis for mixed-method evaluations.

The answers to the four questions lead to two situations in which a mixed-method design would be chosen. The first situation is *satisficing.* In this situation, an ideal mono-method design may not be possible, for practical, contextual, or consequential reasons, but a mixed-method design will be good enough for evaluation purposes (see, for example, Firestone, 1990; Yin, 1994). The second situation is *better-than,* in which mixed-method designs may be the best or only way to go.

Three mixed-method evaluations illustrate how, from the perspective of pragmatic theory, the evaluation decisions did in two instances and did not in one instance yield good consequences. The first is an example of a satisficing situation. The second illustrates an apparently better-than situation that did not work. In describing the second study, I have blurred some details not relevant to the methodological points to avoid what could seem like personal criticism of colleagues who have tried so hard to do a first-rate, pathbreaking evaluation. The third study illustrates a better-than (only-way-to-go) situation that did work.

## A Satisficing Situation: The Indonesia Child Survival Evaluation

In about 1984, the Agency for International Development (AID) decided to expand a program of child survival activities in countries around the world. About three years into the five-year projects, the agency sought a midpoint reading on the achievements and impact of the efforts. The evaluation approach was generally similar in all the national efforts. The Indonesian Child Survival Evaluation is particularly interesting in the adroitness with which the mixed-method design was used to satisfice in an exceptionally challenging context (Dichter, White, Johnson, and Alterman, 1989).

**Pragmatic Considerations.** One of the methodological challenges was detecting change, since the expanded initiatives continued support of four already ongoing activities. These were: immunization; control of diarrheal diseases; improved nutrition through growth monitoring, Vitamin A supplements, and nutrition education; and maternal and child welfare, particularly efforts seeking to decrease high-risk births. Another challenge was attribution, because some aspects of the activities were funded by other donors and because other changes in the nation could have accelerated or delayed improved results.

The practical demands of the evaluation included only a short time on-site (three weeks), a small evaluation team (four persons), and little time for writing up the report. Furthermore, Indonesia, the fifth most populous nation in the world, has 175 million people. They live on about six thousand islands dispersed over an oceanic area about three thousand miles wide and one thousand miles long. These geographic facts affect both program implementation and evaluation opportunities.

An ideal design, for purposes of attribution, would probably have been either a time series or a cohort design in which the innovations were introduced in various combinations in the different islands. Neither of these designs was possible, however, due to practical and contextual circumstances. The evaluators were able, nonetheless, to satisfice in answering evaluative questions, using a mixed-method approach.

**The Design.** Table 3.1 summarizes the evaluation questions and the methods used to answer them. Among the approaches used in this mixed-method design were qualitative document analysis, interviews, quasi-experi-

mental comparisons, and time series analysis, both of the latter involving secondary analysis. Documents included proposals, earlier evaluations by AID,
earlier evaluations by others, research reports from relevant projects in Indonesia and elsewhere on child survival, and documents from relevant ministries.
Data sources included local hospitals, surveys by the Ministry of Health, studies by UNICEF, and surveys conducted by third parties.

Throughout the report, the evaluators note the limitations in confidence
and completeness resulting from this satisficing design. For example, although
child survival was the focus of the AID initiative, national mortality data were
difficult to obtain and interpret. Reaching beyond such existing data, the evaluators found that while experts agreed child mortality was declining, there was
considerable disagreement on how rapidly rates declined and what accounted
for these changes. Time and resources forced reliance on what the evaluators
believed were the most knowledgeable informants.

**Practical Consequences.** Despite these and other limitations, many of
which the evaluators have stated, the report succeeds in giving credible answers
to the evaluation questions within the practical constraints of resources. Design
trade-offs seem optimized, assuming the nonnegotiability of the "four persons,
three weeks" mandate. A large part of the report's success is the adroitness with
which information from many sources was cleverly sought out and stitched
together. Particular care was taken to rule out competing explanations for both
changes and lack of change.

Such a satisficing design does not always work out. All of the other country reports in this child survival evaluation series, completed under the same
constraints but by different evaluation teams for each country, used mixed-
method designs for the same reasons as the Indonesian study. In less skilled
hands, or perhaps the hands of those with little opportunity for rich comparisons and analyses, the results were less satisfying. Some reports, for example,
are little more than descriptions of the country, its history of child health services, and the context for the AID project, with a few qualitative interviews and
simple time series data. In these reports, little information was given on the
basis for interviewee selection, the strengths or limitations of available data,
and competing explanations of what happened.

## A Best-Way Mixed-Method Design: The Comprehensive School Reform Evaluation

Looking back, with the consequences of the evaluation decisions as a pragmatic guide, one sees that several mixed-method evaluations have fallen
short of expectations. One multimillion dollar national study, for example,
on a highly visible mental health demonstration program was designed to
the nth degree of methodological sophistication as a true randomized design.
Extensive care was taken to anticipate issues such as attrition and to select
the finest of statistical fixes. The design called for a blend of detailed implementation studies; cross-site comparisons for experimental and control groups

## Table 3.1. Evaluation Questions and Methods:
## The Indonesian Child Survival Evaluation

| Evaluation Question | Method |
| --- | --- |
| What is the context of the AID effort? What are the AID-unique contributions? | *Historical analysis,* through documents, interviews, and previous reports. |
| | *Qualitative case study description* of probable contributions of changes in rice self-sufficiency, decline in poverty, and increase in education. |
| Overall, how does Indonesia compare to other Asian countries? | *Secondary analysis* of World Bank data. |
| How are the activities being implemented? | *Qualitative document analysis and interviews.* |
| What are the program impacts on services for mothers and children? | *Time series comparisons* using national data on family planning and children's nutritional status. |
| | *Qualitative analysis* of end-of-specific-project reports. |
| What are the program impacts on immunization? | *Time series comparison* using Ministry of Health data and data from another AID project on coverage for DPT1, Polio 1, BCG, measles, and neonatal tetanus. |
| | *Qualitative analysis* of Ministry of Health data on infrastructure changes, such as establishing a cold chain from central to peripheral levels to keep vaccines potent. |
| | *Qualitative case study chain-of-events analysis* linking successful vaccine delivery to establishment of local health clinics (*posyandus*). |
| What are the impacts on health services efficiency? | *Comparative analysis* of unpublished time series vaccine production data showing improvement in coverage equity from 1985 to 1986 and from 1988 to 1989 in urban and rural areas. |
| What are the impacts on infant and child mortality? | *Quasi-experimental comparative pre- and post-analysis* in districts with and without programs, for diseases targeted and not targeted by the interventions, using local area data from hospital records. (Inferences were notably strengthened by the lack of changes in diseases not targeted in both served and unserved communities.) |

on a wide variety of self-report, counselor report, administrative, and other assessment data; qualitative case studies of selected sites; and individual site-specific evaluations carried out by some of the best and the brightest in our profession. At the initiation stage, the study was in the spotlight as the ultimate in contemporary evaluation design that used mixed methods as the best choice.

Now, some years later at the findings stage, the spotlight has been turned off. Some reports have emerged from this study. However, the anticipated final and more comprehensive reports have been delayed by several years. The cost overruns were high. Some staff members have burned out, and the study has become a management Excedrin headache. The anticipated blend of implementation, randomized experiment, case studies, survey, and site-specific evaluations seems to have not met expectations.

In this instance, a better result might have been achieved with a mono-method design, in which evaluators would have answered fewer questions well. Applying the four pragmatic questions, we see that the mixed-method design was able to answer the evaluation questions (OK on criterion 1); overextended the resources of time, money, and staff (not OK on criterion 2); was not necessarily optimal in allocating resources across design trade-offs (not OK on criterion 3); and therefore did not achieve the intended usefulness (not OK on criterion 4). Since the evaluators seemed to favor the randomized experiment, in the sense that results from this experiment were reported and the methodological lessons learned about experimentation were presented, a better choice might have been to use only this experimental design.

**Pragmatic Considerations.** Looking ahead at another best-choice, mixed-method design, we see that a similar situation may arise with a statewide evaluation of a high-visibility school reform demonstration program. The resources proposed for this five-year, ten-district, multischool, multichild study are four full-time evaluator equivalents.

**The Design.** The design of this study is summarized in Table 3.2. The problems that may arise are similar to those just described. The comments illustrate the prospective use of the four pragmatic questions.

**Practical Consequences.** When one applies the four pragmatic questions, this design looks as if it could credibly answer the evaluation questions (OK on criterion 1), although some of the data analysis questions associated with the complex nested design may prove analytically more difficult than anticipated in the proposal. It is not clear that the mixed-method design optimizes resources. The feasibility of completing all the evaluative tasks well, on time, and with the resources available seems like Mission Almost Impossible (not OK on 2). All of the elements in the design may not be necessary for answering the evaluation questions (dubious on 3). This, in turn, could cascade into questions about the evaluation's usefulness to the decision makers (dubious on 4). A better alternative, since case studies seem to be the favored method for these evaluators, might be focusing on those evaluation questions for which case studies are proposed.

## Table 3.2. Evaluation Questions and Methods: Statewide School Reform Evaluation

| Evaluation Question | Method |
| --- | --- |
| What is the baseline of organizational structures and programs to which the experimental programs can be compared? | *Qualitative and quantitative document or record analysis,* including: community-level economic records; administrative data, such as staffing patterns and school district funding; archival records, such as parent notifications. |
| | *Interviews and focus groups* with samples from all ten to fifteen groups affected by the changes. |
| What is progress of implementation? | *Interviews* of members of the affected groups, with samples at state, district, and school levels. |
| | *Document tracking* of formal documents, such as policy statements, and less formal documents, such as meeting announcements. |
| | *Surveys* to assess technical assistance needs. |
| | In-depth *case studies* of selected sites. |
| What are the changes at the district level? | *Interviews and focus groups* with members of the affected groups. |
| | *Observations* of meetings of district planning teams. |
| | *Document analysis* of agendas and meetings minutes. |
| What are the changes at the school and classroom levels? | *Interviews* with members of the affected groups. |
| | *Document or record analysis* of meetings, and administrative records analysis, such as assignment and referral records. |
| | *Classroom observations* of changes, including "shadowing" specific relevant members of affected groups. |
| | In-depth *case studies* of selected individuals. |
| What are the costs and benefits of the changes? | *Cost-benefit analyses* for ten districts, including (1) comparison districts and (2) districts as their own baselines, and including district, school, teacher, and individual student levels of analysis. |

| | |
|---|---|
| How effective and valid is each demonstration district's self-evaluation process? | *Technical reviews* of survey instruments and sampling design. |
| | Administration's *observations* of the in-house evaluation instruments. |
| | *Interviews* to assess stakeholder participation in self-evaluation designs. |
| What is the comparative impact of reforms at districtwide versus school-based levels? | *Comparative analysis* on all of the above questions for school-based and districtwide initiatives. |
| | *Integration* of in-depth case studies. |

## An Only-Way Situation: The H-2A Farmworkers Protection Evaluation

In this study, the mixed-method evaluation design was not developed as satisficing for challenging conditions, but as the only way to answer the evaluation questions. It illustrates that in some instances, mixed methods can pragmatically do a better job than mono-method approaches.

**Pragmatic Considerations.** The H-2A program permits U.S. growers of certain, highly perishable crops, such as apples and tobacco, to hire temporary farmworkers from other countries. To do so, the growers must obtain a permit from the Department of Agriculture, based on evidence that there are no U.S. citizens or legal immigrants available to pick the crops. The growers are required to pay prevailing piece-rate and hourly wages, as appropriate for the crop, and to fulfill other conditions, as well. The intent is to assure that there will be no adverse effects on the employment, wages, and working conditions of U.S. citizens and legal immigrants.

The evaluation questions dealt with whether the H-2A program succeeded in protecting these citizens and legal immigrants. The evaluators' primary concern in designing the study was that the evaluation questions be answered as thoroughly and convincingly as possible. While the report was needed for hearings on changes in immigration law, time and resources were not overwhelming constraints.

**The Design.** Answering the questions as convincingly as possible required an understanding of the program's history and context. Attaining this understanding meant thoroughly evaluating the quality of the data used to establish need, prevailing wages, and hourly wages. Also required was a review of the match between the process as established in legislation, regulations, and procedures, and the process as it happened "on the farm," along with evidence of how well these procedures, if properly carried out, actually protected U.S. and legal immigrant farmworkers (U.S. Government Accounting Office, 1989).

Table 3.3 presents the evaluation questions and the mixed-method design developed to answer these questions. The methods include an ethnographic case study, historical analysis, field test of worker availability, technical reviews, and secondary analysis of wage data. To implement this mixed-method design, the evaluation team included a highly experienced agricultural ethnographer, a labor economist, a survey researcher, and staff members who were fluent bilinguals in the various dialects of the workers, both resident and temporary.

**Practical Consequences.** The results of the evaluation underscored the pragmatic necessity of using mixed methods. With regard to the trustworthiness of key wage data (the second set of evaluation questions in Table 3.3), combining scrutiny of agency methodology with participant-observer analysis of process showed important, but fixable, flaws in design with considerable erosion of survey quality in the field. For example, on some occasions, the stratified random sampling designs selected in Washington turned out to be convenience samples in practice. Further erosion of quality was found in survey data collection errors and coding errors, leading to underestimates of statistical error and misleadingly precise data. These problems, too, were seen as fixable.

The interview, document analysis, and empirical checks on farm job advertising and worker responses showed that the letter of the H-2A law was being followed, but not the spirit. That is, as legally required, the relevant offices accepted the applications for H-2A permits, which were technically complete, and the employment agency referral process was followed. On paper, the protections would seem to have been working. However, the spirit of the law was missing. The observations indicated that the reviews, advertising, and referrals were pro forma, rather than a vigorous effort to promote the employment of U.S. and legal immigrant workers.

Furthermore, the ethnographic case studies revealed the dynamics underlying the compliance-oriented pattern. U.S. and legal immigrant workers in the area were mostly women and older persons. They were perceived by growers as being less productive and more difficult to train and manage than the H-2A workers. A system had developed over the years between growers and a legal immigrant worker with connections in villages in his own country. The farmers would let this worker know how many field hands they needed, and when. This worker contacted his village connections and energetic young men went north. A good, steady supply of trained, hale, uncomplaining workers was assured. Local workers expected that they might be nominally hired, but their lives would be pretty miserable. For example, they might be assigned the hardest possible work, such as mucking out barns. In some instances, physical fights with the growers were reported. For these reasons, local workers looked elsewhere. A door-to-door survey by the Government Accounting Office (GAO) ethnographers showed that few local workers would apply for the tobacco jobs. They took alternate employment available to them.

Adjacent to the county selected for the intensive case study there was a very similar tobacco growing area with a low H-2A application rate. Informants in this county told GAO that the reason for the lower rate was not that working conditions were better and that U.S. and legal immigrant workers filled the jobs, but that allegedly illegal fieldworkers were employed. While

## Table 3.3. Evaluation Questions and Methods: The H-2A Farmworkers Study

| Evaluation Question | Method |
|---|---|
| What is the history of the H-2A program? How does this program relate to previous and current farmworker immigration policies? | *Historical analysis* of legislation, regulations, prior research, and evaluation reports. |
| | *Interviews* with federal and state officials and with agricultural labor experts. |
| | *Expert panel analyses.* |
| Are the key data required to carry out this program trustworthy? | In-depth *case study* of all aspects of the design, collection, coding, quality control, analysis, and reporting of national and state databases. Study included review by survey research experts, independent quality check of the databases, and participant observation. |
| How does the process on paper compare with the process in the field? | *Interviews, document analysis,* and in-depth *case studies* at selected sites of the process during a growing and harvesting season. |
| | *Survey* of representative field offices. |
| Do the provisions in the H-2A program succeed in protecting U.S. and legal farmworkers' employment opportunities, wages, and working conditions? | *Secondary analysis* of employment and wage information. |
| | In-depth *ethnographic comparative case study* in tobacco industry. |
| | *Ethnographic case studies* for selected other crops. |
| What are alternate explanations for the apparent lack of U.S. and legal farmworkers? | In case study sites, *interviews, analysis* of employment histories, and *door-to-door tests* of worker availability. |

the case study county response to the law was one of surface compliance, the comparison county's response was—allegedly—to break the law. It seemed unlikely this information could have been obtained through document analysis, traditional survey research, or interviews. The ethnographic case study and participant-observer methodology was essential for the in-depth understanding sought in the evaluation.

This application of mixed methods was not without its problems (Datta, 1996). First, evaluation management decisions took much more time than anticipated when trade-offs had to be made between methodologies as the study progressed. Second, there was a large learning curve in meshing ethnographic information with an evaluation environment requiring audit-trail quality data and referencing for quality assurance. Third, it was difficult to retain the rich interpretation and analysis when the key ethnographer accepted a well-deserved, high-level position in another agency. This somewhat constrained the fullest use of the mixed-method results in the final report.

In the H-2A study, therefore, the particular mix of methods chosen passed the pragmatic tests of answering the questions credibly, optimizing design trade-offs, and promoting useful understanding. The mix was less successful in implementation because of its dependence on particular staff abilities.

## The Pragmatic Basis for Mixed-Method Designs in Some Current Thinking

A pragmatist's approach to mixed-method design, as presented here, requires systematic consideration of practicality, contextual responsiveness, and con-sequentiality. This calls for information that is rarely available in the formal lit-erature. For the approach to work well, beyond cumulation of individual evaluator or team trial-and-error, we need to share more experiences about the practical consequences of design decisions. There are some exceptionally valuable self-reports on how a decision (such as the choice of a randomized design) worked out in practice (see, for example, Conrad, 1994). Further-more, particularly in the mid-1970s and early 1980s, there was an extensive, and on the whole methodologically fruitful, dialog in critiquing national eval-uations such as the Westinghouse-Ohio quasi-experimental study of Head Start, the Sesame Street evaluation, the evaluation of the New Jersey negative income tax experiment, and others. More recently, however, after completion and publication of the reports, it is relatively hard to find published detailed critiques—both of the large national studies and the much more numerous state and local evaluations.

The critiques, again quite fruitfully, tend to be on broader issues, such as those rooted in concerns for social justice and the role of evaluation. To make a pragmatic basis for mixed-method designs fully workable, a body of knowledge would have to be developed on the practical, contextual, and par-ticularly consequential results of diverse mixed-method evaluations. Nonetheless, it seems both feasible and useful to apply pragmatic theory to program evaluation—both prospectively and as the sharing of experience continues—to the place in which the test of pragmatic truth is found: in the consequences of the evaluative decisions.

Several evaluation texts draw on the use of decision-oriented, utilization-oriented, and other practical approaches, for example, in the *Evaluator's Hand-book* (Herman, Morris, and Fitz-Gibbon, 1987). The more recent *Handbook of Practical Evaluation* (Wholey, Hatry, and Newcomer, 1994) presents at length a pragmatic approach to methodology in evaluation design (qualitative and quantitative), practical data collection procedures, practical data analysis, and planning and managing evaluation for maximum effectiveness.

Other evaluation theorists contest the preferential valuing of the practical in these texts. In his provocative discussion, which uses Wholey, Hatry, and Newcomer's *Handbook of Practical Evaluation* (1994) as a case in point, Scriven (1996) raises the question of the relation of theory to practice in evaluation. He examines two questions: Whether or to what extent "practical evaluation, especially practical program evaluation, depends on theoretical assumptions that puts its procedures and conclusions at risk . . . and [the extent to which] practical evaluation is unnecessarily and seriously limited because of its failure to use theory as a way to recognize and develop solutions to new problems" (p. 393).

It should be clear that, in the current discussion of the pragmatic basis of mixed-method design, the issues considered fall in the area Scriven considers important but not highly theory-dependent, such as data access and the match of design to context. The areas that he effectively argues to be extremely important, such as the logic of evaluation that helps to define what types of study (policies, products, personnel) are included in our field, have not been discussed in this chapter. However, the approach that has been presented—giving design decisions a pragmatic basis—does not preclude attention to what Scriven describes as low-level theory. Moreover, if one envisions evaluation theory as more centrally oriented around the definition that evaluation is the study of the merit (or quality), worth (or value), or significance of various entities, one sees that the practical and pragmatic considerations presented here are highly relevant and of great potential value to theorists and practitioners alike.

## References

Chen, H.-T. *Evaluation Theory*. Thousand Oaks, Calif.: Sage, 1992.

Conrad, K. J. *Critically Evaluating the Role of Experiments*. New Directions for Program Evaluation, no. 63. San Francisco: Jossey-Bass, 1994.

Datta, L. "Mixed-Method Evaluations." In E. Chelimsky and W. R. Shadish (eds.), *Program Evaluation*. Thousand Oaks, Calif.: Sage, 1996.

Dichter, P., White, W., Johnson, P., and Alterman, D. *Child Survival in Indonesia*. Impact Evaluation no. 75. Washington, D.C.: U.S. Agency for International Development, 1989.

Firestone, W. A. "Accommodation: Toward a Paradigm-Praxis Dialectic." In E. G. Guba (ed.), *The Paradigm Dialog*. Thousand Oaks, Calif.: Sage, 1990.

Herman, J., Morris, L., and Fitz-Gibbon, C. *Evaluator's Handbook*. (2nd ed.) Thousand Oaks, Calif.: Sage, 1987.

Patton, M. Q. "Paradigms and Pragmatism." In D. M. Fetterman (ed.), *Qualitative Approaches to Evaluation in Education: The Silent Scientific Revolution*. New York: Praeger, 1988.

Patton, M. Q. *Qualitative Evaluation and Research Methods*. (2nd ed.) Thousand Oaks, Calif.: Sage, 1990.

Schwandt, T. A. "Paths to Inquiry in the Social Disciplines: Scientific, Constructivist, and Critical Theory Methodologies." In E. G. Guba (ed.), *The Paradigm Dialog*. Thousand Oaks, Calif.: Sage, 1990.

Scriven, M. *The Evaluation Thesaurus*. Thousand Oaks, Calif.: Sage, 1990.

Scriven, M. "The Theory Behind Practical Evaluation." *Evaluation*, 1996, 2 (4), 393–404.

Shadish, W. R., Newman, D., Scheirer, M. A., and Wye, C. *Guiding Principles for Evaluators*. New Directions for Evaluation, no. 66. San Francisco: Jossey-Bass, 1995.

Skrtic, T. M. "Social Accommodation: Toward a Dialogical Discourse on Educational Inquiry." In E. G. Guba (ed.), *The Paradigm Dialog*. Thousand Oaks, Calif.: Sage, 1990.

U.S. General Accounting Office. *The H-2A Program: Protections for U.S. Farmworkers*. (PEMD-89–3) Washington, D.C.: U.S. General Accounting Office, 1989.

U.S. General Accounting Office. *Cross Design Synthesis: A New Strategy for Medical Effectiveness Research*. (PEMD-92–18) Washington, D.C.: U.S. General Accounting Office, 1992.

Wholey, J. S., Hatry, H., and Newcomer, K. *Handbook of Practical Evaluation*. Thousand Oaks, Calif.: Sage, 1994.

Yin, R. K. *Case Study Research: Design and Methods*. (2nd ed.) Thousand Oaks, Calif.: Sage, 1994.

*LOIS-ELLIN DATTA is president of Datta Analysis. Previously, she was director of program evaluation in the Human Services Division at the U.S. General Accounting Office and editor-in-chief of* New Directions for Evaluation. *She has been involved in designing, implementing, and thinking about mixed-method and mono-method designs in such areas as tax expenditures, health care policy, housing, and child development.*

*A review of qualitative methods used in a predominantly quantitative evaluation indicated a variety of roles for such a mixing of methods, including framing initial questions and method choices, revising evaluation questions during the inquiry, assessing the validity of measures, assessing adaptations in program implementation, and gauging the proper degree of uncertainty and generalizability of one's conclusions. These functions are considered in light of the stances on mixing paradigms that Greene and Caracelli describe in Chapter One.*

# Integrating Qualitative Methods in a Predominantly Quantitative Evaluation: A Case Study and Some Reflections

*Melvin M. Mark, Irwin Feller, Scott B. Button*

Recent years have seen ongoing debate about the relative merits of qualitative and quantitative approaches in many of the social sciences. Discussions of qualitative and quantitative paradigms and methods are commonplace in the program evaluation literature, and have ranged in tone from conciliatory and integrative (for example, Reichardt and Cook, 1979; Greene, Caracelli, and Graham, 1989) to confrontative and separatist (for example, Lincoln, 1991; Sechrest, 1992). Although a consensus has not yet emerged, there appears to be a growing feeling among many that continued debate about qualitative *versus* quantitative approaches is increasingly unproductive, and that we should instead focus on doing the work of evaluation well (Datta, 1994; House, 1994).

The chapters in this volume attempt to contribute to this end by addressing the potential and challenges of integrating different methods in an evaluation. Few extended examples of such integration have been presented in the literature. Moreover, there is a paucity of examples that focus on the integration of qualitative methods in evaluations that employ a predominantly quantitative framework. Such an example is the corpus of this chapter and provides a springboard to some observations about mixed-method designs.

The absence of detailed discussions of the role of qualitative methods in predominantly quantitative evaluations has contributed to several problems in the literature. First, it has contributed to inaccurate characterizations of quantitative evaluations, for example, as positivist and inherently distant from the phenomenon being studied. Second, the lack of focus on the role of qualitative methods in many quantitative evaluations has probably led to an underestimate of the frequency with which multiple methods are used (compare Caracelli and Greene, 1993). Third, the failure to detail the mixed-method applications may have hindered efforts to describe the various functions that multiple methods can serve (see Greene, Caracelli, and Graham, 1989; Mark and Shotland, 1987).

In this chapter, we describe several ways in which qualitative methods were integrated in a predominantly quantitative evaluation. We then discuss these mixed-method examples in light of Greene and Caracelli's description (Chapter One of this volume) of three stances on mixed methods.

## The USDA Personnel Demonstration Project

The United States Department of Agriculture (USDA) Personnel Management Demonstration Project involved implementing and evaluating an alternative recruitment and selection system for hiring federal employees. The project was carried out in two of USDA's agencies: the Agricultural Research Service (ARS) and the Forest Service (FS). The purpose of the USDA demonstration project was cited in a *Federal Register* notice announcing the project (Department of Agriculture, 1990): "The purpose of this demonstration project is to develop a recruitment and selection program for new hires that is flexible and responsive to local recruitment needs and which will facilitate the attainment of a quality workforce reflective of society" (p. 9065).

The demonstration project was initially predicated in part on the need to overcome the federal government's competitive disadvantages in national labor markets, which were predicted in *Civil Service 2000* (Hudson Institute, 1988) and other reports. Following the initiation of the demonstration project, some of the labor force and demographic projections of *Civil Service 2000* and its predecessor, *Workforce 2000,* were called into question (U.S. General Accounting Office, 1992). In addition, national economic conditions during the early portion of the demonstration project counteracted the labor force projections of *Civil Service 2000* and *Workforce 2000.*

Nevertheless, interest in reforming the federal hiring process appears to have increased. Long-standing concerns about the complexity and slowness of the traditional hiring system persist (National Commission on Public Service, 1989), and calls continue for a "flexible and responsive hiring system" (Gore, 1993, p. 163). The USDA demonstration project, by evaluating a reform designed to increase deregulation and decentralization of the hiring process, has the potential to inform ongoing efforts to reform federal hiring processes.

## Components and Expected Effects of the Demonstration Project

As specified in the *Federal Register* notice of March 9, 1990, the demonstration project consisted of five discrete components or initiatives.

1. The Office of Personnel Management, which oversees federal hiring, gave ARS and FS the authority to determine a "shortage category," that is, an occupation for which there is a known paucity of applicants and for which a simplified hiring process (direct hire authority) was approved.

2. An alternative method was employed to assess applicants for positions. This alternative method grouped job candidates into two categories (quality and eligible), in contrast with the traditional system, which examines, numerically rates, and then ranks candidates. Applicants were assigned to the "quality" group on the basis of above-average educational achievement, job-related quality experience, or high ability. Any candidate assigned to the quality group could be selected for the position. Thus, the quality grouping process did not include the traditional "rule of three," whereby the manager must select from only the three most highly rated candidates. Candidates who did not fall into the quality group but who passed minimum qualification standards were assigned to the "eligible" group. If the quality group were not sufficiently large (for example, not more than one or two candidates), the eligible group could also be referred to the manager.

3. Monetary incentives could be used for recruitment purposes. These incentives could be deferred (up to thirty-six months) or paid as a lump sum upon beginning duty. A twelve-month service agreement was required, with mandatory repayment if the employee did not remain employed for that period.

4. Relocation travel and transportation expenses for travel to the first post of duty could be reimbursed, including all expenses normally offered to transferred employees.

5. The standard one-year probationary period for federal employees was extended to three years for research scientists.

In addition, under the authority granted to the demonstration project, absolute preference was given to veterans. If there were no veterans in a quality group, any candidate could be selected from that group. However, if the quality group contained veterans and nonveterans, a nonveteran could be selected only if all veterans were disqualified. In contrast, in the traditional system, additional points are awarded to veterans. These points improve the individual's rank relative to other candidates. However, the manager selects from the top three available candidates. A veteran must be chosen ahead of all others equal or lower in rank, but not before others who are ranked higher.

As specified in the same *Federal Register* notice, relative to the comparison group, the demonstration group was expected to show certain outcomes, including:

- Reports by managers of greater responsiveness to local recruitment needs
- Greater managerial satisfaction with the qualification of candidates
- Greater responsibility felt by managers for recruitment success
- No increase in staff time devoted to hiring
- Decreased intervals between a vacancy announcement and a job offer

- At a minimum, no decrease in the quality of applicants in terms of educational achievement, quality of experience, or professional achievements
- No negative impact on recruiting research scientists due to the extension of their probationary period

## Evaluation Framework: Design and Data Sources

The basic framework of the USDA demonstration project evaluation employed traditional quantitative methods. Research sites were randomly assigned (within constraints) to the demonstration project hiring system and the traditional hiring system to facilitate inferences about the impact of the new system. The constraints were set so as to optimize the expected level of usage of the demonstration hiring system, especially in job categories identified by the agencies as difficult to fill, up to the authorized level of 5,000 demonstration hires. Of the 222 local administrative units, or sites, involved, 141 used the demonstration hiring system, while 81 continued to use standard recruitment and selection methods.

The critical outcome variables were measured quantitatively. Some outcome variables were taken from standard and specially constructed databases that contained information about personnel actions, including the applicants and people selected for each vacancy. Other variables were measured in surveys of managers and of applicants. The outcome variables included the number of applicants for a position, the number of days needed to fill a position, the demographic characteristics of new employees, and managers' satisfaction with the hiring system.

Although the fundamental evaluation design was quantitative, qualitative components were included from the beginning. The major qualitative component was carried out each year of the evaluation in a series of site visits that included interviews with managers, personnel specialists, and selected employees, as well as observations and file reviews. During the five years of the evaluation, ninety-six site visits were conducted and forty-five separate sites were visited. These site visits and other qualitative aspects of the evaluation contributed to the evaluation in several ways, many of which are summarized below. Further detail about the evaluation design, research procedures, analyses, and data sources is available in Mark and others (1995).

## Contributions of Qualitative Methods in the USDA Demonstration Evaluation

In this section, we describe several functions that qualitative methods served in the predominantly quantitative USDA demonstration project. We then address the evaluation in terms of the three stances on mixed methods that Greene and Caracelli describe in Chapter One of this volume. Our description of various functions that mixed methods serve is not novel, and it overlaps with prior statements by Cook and Reichardt (1979); Greene, Caracelli, and Graham (1989); Hedrick (1994); Mark and Shotland (1987); and others.

**Framing the Research Question or Quantitative Method.** A number of authors have suggested that quantitative outcome evaluations be preceded by a variety of qualitative activities. For example, evaluability assessment (Wholey, 1987) and program theory development (Bickman, 1990) require interviews, observations, and document review.

Several aspects of the USDA demonstration project evaluation illustrate the use of qualitative methods to develop quantitative procedures. For example, the evaluation included survey instruments designed for different groups, such as an annual survey of managers. Sponsors of the USDA demonstration project hypothesized that the demonstration hiring system would be associated with higher managerial satisfaction, relative to the traditional system. The survey also assessed managers' perceptions of such outcomes as hiring speed and responsiveness of the hiring process to local hiring needs.

Several qualitative activities were employed in developing this measure. A model of the hiring process was developed from agency and other federal documents and tested against files of actual hirings and against on-site observations and interviews. Focus groups were conducted with program staff and personnel specialists to identify appropriate outcomes, as well as to learn the jargon that respondents use. Managers read drafts of the survey, discussed their interpretations of outcomes, and suggested additions and deletions. These procedures led to revisions of almost three-fourths of the original items.

We do not believe that the efforts underlying the development of our surveys were exceptional. To the contrary, we believe that most quantitative evaluators employ many of the same procedures, in varying degrees of formality, to develop instruments and frame research questions (Hedrick, 1994). As Campbell (1974) pointed out, quantitative methods are based on qualitative knowledge. Detailed qualitative underpinnings of quantitative methods also help avoid a problem that some critics of quantitative approaches cite, namely that such methods are more distant from the phenomenon under investigation (Guba and Lincoln, 1989) and less responsive to stakeholders' concerns.

**Serving as a Validity Check.** Managerial satisfaction with the demonstration hiring system was assessed both through the quantitative survey and through interviews during site visits. If the two provided convergent evidence, we could have interpreted the qualitative observations as validating the conclusions from the quantitative procedures. However, there was a discrepancy. Initial findings from the survey of managers revealed statistically significant but extremely modest differences in satisfaction between demonstration and comparison group managers. In contrast, decidedly more satisfaction with the demonstration system was expressed during the site visit interviews. This conflict between the findings of two inquiry modes created a puzzle that demanded resolution. If no convincing resolution is reached, the divergence of findings across inquiry modes should result in more uncertainty about the conclusions. In Reichardt and Gollob's terms (1987), the plausibility bracket widens.

**Reframing the Research Question or Method.** In principle, there were several possible reasons for this discrepancy between the survey of managers and the site visit estimates of managerial satisfaction. However, qualitative findings from the first years of site visits suggested that, because of a measurement problem, the survey results underestimated managers' satisfaction with the demonstration hiring system. The initial manager survey included a large number of items worded generically with terms such as "hiring system." Items were constructed in this generic fashion so that identical items could be answered by both demonstration and comparison site managers. However, we found in the first year of site visits that in responding to questions about the "hiring system," managers often included other personnel functions, particularly classification (how jobs are defined, titled, and located in the system that determines pay ranges) and compensation (what people are paid). For this and other reasons, the manager survey was revised, with fewer items overall and with numerous items that specifically addressed either the demonstration hiring authority or the standard hiring authorities.

With the revised manager survey items, the discrepancy between the site visit interviews and the survey results essentially disappeared. Moreover, analyses across survey items supported the interpretation generated from the site visit interviews—that the original discrepancy had resulted from the generic wording used in the first survey instrument. Larger survey differences were obtained when questions implicitly or explicitly contrasted the demonstration hiring authority with the standard hiring procedures, while smaller differences emerged on items with more generic wording.

**Improving Communication of Quantitative Findings.** Several researchers have noted the value of how qualitative observations "flesh out" quantitative findings (for example, Hedrick, 1994). The addition of participants' comments or of observations can help communicate quantitative findings, especially to audiences not used to statistical presentations. Consider, for example, one manager's statement about the demonstration project, or "demo": "Demo is easier than we anticipated. It allows us to avoid the 'paperwork nightmare.' Demo is simple. Demo works so well!" Such a quote can convey far more information to many stakeholders than can the result of a multivariate test.

**Explaining Quantitative Findings.** The demonstration project allowed the option of cash recruitment incentives. This component was designed to "increase the flexibility and responsiveness of the recruitment and hiring system" (U.S. Department of Agriculture, 1990, p. 9067), and to enhance the competitiveness of the federal government in vying with other employers for qualified applicants.

Findings indicated that the recruitment incentives component of the demonstration project was used very infrequently. During interviews, respondents offered several explanations for the limited use of incentives, including (1) an economic recession early in the project that reportedly increased the pool of qualified applicants, (2) hiring freezes in the agencies later in the project, (3) site-specific layoffs by particular employers (for example, defense-related employers) that were credited with increasing the availability of certain types of applicants, and (4) concern by some selecting officials and person-nelists that injudicious use of cash recruitment incentives could create equity concerns among current employees. (As an aside, findings from case study site visits suggested that although financial incentives were used infrequently, they were important factors in specific cases.)

For the findings regarding recruitment incentives and for many other find-ings, the qualitative observations were critical in providing explanations. More generally, it is useful to know *why* interventions succeed or fail (Lipsey, 1993), and explanations of program success or failure are likely to be facilitated through the use of qualitative methods.

**Studying Context and Probing the Limits of Generalizability.** The site visit findings also provided reason for caution in generalizing from the quan-titative results on the use of recruitment incentives to other periods of time with different labor market conditions. The qualitative site visits indicated that it is conceivable that recruitment incentives, especially cash incentives, might be used substantially more often and may be more important to successful recruiting in a more competitive labor market.

More generally, qualitative observations revealed several important factors for understanding the context in which the demonstration hiring authority was implemented. These factors are also important in considering the generaliz-ability of the quantitative findings to other settings and times (Cronbach, 1982). For instance, in telling their stories of recruitment and selection, managers and new employees indicated the importance of classification, pay, the labor mar-ket conditions, and hiring restrictions. Take, as an example, pay. For particular occupations and in particular (predominantly metropolitan) locations, federal pay scales (and opportunities for promotion) are reportedly viewed as less desir-able than alternatives outside the federal sector. Sites report difficulty in hiring for these positions, with the demonstration initiatives seen as having limited efficacy in overcoming such difficulties. Alternatively, if the federal pay scale for a position were considerably higher than that outside the federal sector, a sim-pler hiring system would probably not be needed. This example and several other observations from the qualitative component of the evaluation point to the need for caution in generalizing findings to future conditions should a rel-evant factor (for example, pay) change.

**Studying Implementation Processes and Adaptations.** During site visit interviews at demonstration sites, particularly early visits, many respondents expressed dissatisfaction with the criteria used to admit applicants to the qual-ity group (that is, the group of applicants automatically referred to the select-ing official as eligible for selection). Respondents sometimes questioned why specific individuals, whom they believed to be inappropriate for the job, were included in the quality group.

Efforts to address such problems were evident during the later rounds of case study site visits. In particular, attention to the specification of "selective placement factors" increased at many demonstration sites. Used in conjunction with the general qualification standards, these factors define the minimum knowledge, skills, and abilities required to perform the duties of a position. Selective placement factors thereby function as job-relevant criteria against which applicants are evaluated.

The qualitative observations and interviews conducted during the site visits allowed us to gain insight into the increased importance that many managers and personnelists assigned to selective placement factors as the implementation of the demonstration hiring system continued. They also provided a window into how selective placement factors were identified and, more generally, how the demonstration hiring system worked.

A mixed-method approach may allow evaluators to study implementation processes better (Hedrick, 1994; Reichardt and Cook, 1979), including "learning-by-using," whereby program personnel improve ways of applying the intervention. Mixed methods may also be useful in identifying implementation problems, such as the failure to employ the program as designed.

**Probing Emerging Questions.** During the life of the USDA demonstration project, increasing national attention was given to reforming a wide range of federal processes, including hiring (DiIulio, 1994; Gore, 1993). Calls for reform typically suggested both deregulation and decentralization of authority. The demonstration project can be described in terms of these two characteristics. It involves deregulation in that it permits flexibilities not present in the traditional hiring system. For example, categorical grouping replaces the traditional rating and ranking procedures. Moreover, in the demonstration hiring authority, the traditional rule of three, whereby a manager must select from among the three most highly rated candidates, does not apply. The demonstration hiring system also involves decentralization, in that authorities are delegated from the Office of Personnel Management (OPM) to the agencies, and hiring practices that the centralized OPM might have carried out are instead implemented by the agencies.

With this increasing attention to decentralization and deregulation, we began to wonder whether the effects of the demonstration hiring authority are due to decentralization, deregulation, both, or neither. The question has possible policy implications, in that it is possible to decentralize standard hiring practices without deregulating, and it is likewise possible to deregulate without decentralizing.

Although the demonstration project was not designed to address directly whether the demonstration project effects depended on decentralization or on deregulation, we explored this issue in considerable detail during the last year's site visits. The site visit results, along with convergent evidence from specially designed survey items, suggested that the deregulated policies and procedures embodied in the demonstration project are at least as important as, and probably more important than, decentralization in bringing about the effects of the demonstration project. Of course, different forms of deregulation would have different results, and the effects and side effects of any deregulation may depend on the accountability, oversight, and monitoring processes that accompany it.

The point for evaluation practice is that quantitative summative evaluations are designed to assess the impact and worth of a particular intervention, and it typically remains an open question as to the relevance of the evaluation findings for new or different policy questions (Cronbach, 1982). Supplementing the quantitative evaluation with qualitative methods may allow more flexibility in responding to emerging policy questions.

**Anticipating the Importance of Mixed Methods.** The USDA demonstration project lasted five years. Over such a long period, changes may occur in many areas, including the contextual variables that influence the intervention, the way the intervention is implemented, and the type of policy questions to which evaluation findings might contribute. Given the increased probability of such changes with time, the value of a mixed-method approach is likely to be greater for longer evaluations. Similarly, other factors, such as anticipated changes in political administrations or agency management, may foreshadow the kind of shifts—such as a change in which policy questions are of interest—that increase the importance of a mixed-method approach.

## The Paradigm Issue

In this final section, we link the methodological strategies we used in the USDA demonstration project evaluation to the mixed-method framework Greene and Caracelli present in Chapter One of this volume. Expanding from these linkages, we then offer our own mixed-method thinking and ideas.

**Three Stances on Mixing Paradigms in Mixed-Method Studies.** Greene and Caracelli (Chapter One of this volume) describe three positions regarding the mixing of paradigms while mixing methods. First, the purist stance holds that different paradigms involve incompatible assumptions (for example, on objectivity versus subjectivity), so that mixing inquiry paradigms is not feasible or sensible. Second, the pragmatist position acknowledges philosophical differences across inquiry paradigms, but sees these as weakly linked to the practice of inquiry and as secondary to the demands of a particular research question. The pragmatist stance is that researchers should select whatever works best, which will commonly include a mixture of methods, given the complexity of social phenomena. Third, the dialectical stance holds that paradigm differences are important, and that it is through a synthesis across different method types that richer and more accurate understandings emerge. Greene and Caracelli suggest two possible groundings for dialectical mixed-method inquiry. The first is a set of characteristics seen as associated with qualitative and quantitative modes of inquiry, respectively, such as particularity versus generality, closeness versus distance, and meaning versus causality. Greene and Caracelli note that mixed-method designs can fruitfully strive to combine the characteristics of different inquiry traditions, resulting for example in inferences grounded in participants' lives but with credible claims about generalizability. A second grounding that Greene and Caracelli suggest for a dialectical approach involves focusing on a value base, rather than an epistemological base, for social inquiry. That value base includes a concern for community and practical action; the choice of mixed methods is likely to be based on values rather than methodological concerns.

**The Paradigm Issue and the USDA Demonstration Project.** How do the various uses of qualitative methods in the USDA demonstration project relate to the paradigm issue as described by Greene and Caracelli? Clearly the mixed-method design of this evaluation does not correspond to the purist stance, which holds that because of paradigm incompatibility, mixing inquiry paradigms is not feasible or sensible. But does the evaluation follow the pragmatist or the dialectical stance?

At first glance, the USDA demonstration project appears to be a clear example of the pragmatist stance. Qualitative approaches were used to conduct tasks for which they seemed better suited than quantitative methods, such as identifying important contextual factors and adaptations in the implementation process. Qualitative methods seemed better suited for these tasks given that the phenomena under study occur in "open systems," in which unanticipated changes can occur. Qualitative methods were also used in the service of quantitative methods, for example to frame and reframe quantitative methods, to assess the validity of quantitative methods, and to aid in their communication and explanation. The design of the evaluation thus appears to be an opportunistic mixing of methods to meet the demands of the inquiry problem in the best way possible.

At the same time, our mixing of methods could be construed as capitalizing on several of the characteristics that Greene and Caracelli identified as typical of quantitative and qualitative methods. In particular, the interviews and observations carried out in the site visits were designed to achieve several of the characteristics Greene and Caracelli noted as being more typical of interpretivistic approaches, such as attaining closeness to the phenomenon, tapping practical wisdom, and providing contextual understanding of local meaning. One could view the inclusion of these more commonly interpretivistic features, along with the features associated with the quantitative design, as an attempt to follow the dialectical stance.

In addition, the early findings with respect to managerial satisfaction indicate the potential for a dialectic to emerge from the mixed methods. The quantitative manager survey initially indicated that demonstration site managers were mildly more satisfied with the recruitment and selection system than were comparison managers. In contrast, the site visits indicated a large difference. The site visit observations had a level of closeness, particularity, and contextualized understanding beyond that of the survey. The discrepancy between the results of the two inquiry methods could have initiated precisely the kind of dialectic that Caracelli and Greene suggested could lead to a richer and more insightful understanding than either method alone.

In fact, the discrepancy between the qualitative case study and quantitative survey results led to improvements of the survey instrument, enhancements that ended the discrepancy. As this example from the demonstration project indicates, the question is empirical: Will the puzzles that mixed methods generate lead to (1) enriched and more insightful understandings; (2) a methodological or logical resolution of conflicting findings, in which the conflict is more apparent than real; or to (3) a conundrum that yields no increased understanding other than caution and more modesty about the conclusions to be drawn? Similarly, the interviews and observations from the site visits *could* have led to conflicting findings and perspectives that would have enriched the evaluation, but this did not happen in practice. In short, productive dialectics sometimes occur and sometimes do not. One strategy, then, is to develop a mixed-method design that allows such a dialectic to emerge and that pragmatically employs the relative strengths of different methods for different contexts in case a productive dialectic does not emerge. Perhaps this mixed stance should be called the pragmatic, potentially dialectical approach.

Another, modest example of a dialectic emerging from mixed methods involves the insight that site visit interviews and observations gave into the nature of the manager-personnelist relations. We briefly alluded to this relationship in our earlier discussion of selective placement factors, which apparently increased in importance as some agency personnel adapted to the demonstration hiring system. More generally, the manager-personnelist relationship appeared to be an important determinant of success in the hiring process. The qualitative components of the evaluation helped "account" for what was "error variance" from the perspective of the quantitative design. Again, the mixed design may be open to the emergence of dialectic, but whether it emerges and, if so, how valuable it is, will vary from evaluation to evaluation.

**Beyond Paradigmatic Conflict.** Much of the literature on qualitative and quantitative approaches has centered on whether there are competing, incompatible paradigms (Reichardt and Cook, 1979; Smith and Heshusius, 1986). The pragmatist and dialectical stances summarized by Greene and Caracelli are strategies for getting beyond paradigmatic conflict, but they appear to assume that qualitative and quantitative paradigms each have integrity and are distinct. Is there not an alternative to continued paradigm-based debate?

The paradigmatic conflict that underlies many discussions of qualitative and quantitative methods is not inevitable (House, 1994). Some form of critical realism (Bhaskar, 1978; House, 1991), such as emergent realism (Henry, Julnes, and Mark, in press), offers promise as a paradigm that embraces both qualitative and quantitative methods, and their integration. Emergent realism, like other forms of critical realism, assumes the existence of an external reality apart from our interpretations of it (unlike some radical forms of constructivism). It also assumes that underlying generative forces exist that lead to some observable regularities, though these regularities are far from perfect given that the underlying relations are complex and poorly understood and occur in open systems. Thus, unlike positivism, emergent realism emphasizes the tentativeness of our observations.

Emergent realists acknowledge that inquiry paradigms with philosophical differences have developed, but see some form of critical realism as an alternative paradigm. Indeed, it can be argued that the whole hue and cry about qualitative and quantitative methods, indeed the paradigm wars themselves, are the result of an accident of history. It was not inevitable that logical positivism would become dominant in the received philosophy of science. Nor was it inevitable that, in part, as a response to the inadequacies of logical positivism, constructivism would become the predominantly visible alternative, or that forms of constructivism would be offered and adopted that eschew the search for causal generalizations. (It is, however, ironic that a philosophy of science that emphasizes localized knowledge and context-boundedness appears to be seen by some of its adherents as universally applicable and not historically bound.)

Thus, the emergent realist perspective denies that there are inevitable paradigm differences associated with qualitative and quantitative modes of inquiry. Like the pragmatist stance, emergent realism holds that researchers should select whatever works best, and that this will commonly include a mixture of methods, given the complexity of social phenomena. Like the dialectical stance, emergent realism holds that a synthesis across different method types will sometimes provide richer and more accurate understandings. From the perspective of emergent realism, however, the dialectical value of different methods results not from their association with different paradigms but from their strengths in probing different aspects of the indirectly observable generative mechanisms associated with social programs, as well as different aspects of the value context in which programs operate (for more detail, see Henry, Julnes, and Mark, in press).

## References

Bhaskar, R. A. *A Realist Theory of Science.* Atlantic Highlands, N.J.: Humanities Press, 1978.

Bickman, L. (ed.). *Advances in Program Theory.* New Directions for Program Evaluation, no. 47. San Francisco: Jossey-Bass, 1990.

Campbell, D. T. "Qualitative Knowing in Action Research." Kurt Lewin Address presented at the annual meeting of the American Psychological Association, New Orleans, Sept. 1974.

Caracelli, V. J., and Greene, J. C. "Data Analysis Strategies for Mixed-Method Evaluation Designs." *Educational Evaluation and Policy Analysis,* 1993, *15* (2), 195–207.

Cook, T. D., and Reichardt, C. S. (eds.). *Qualitative and Quantitative Methods in Evaluation Research.* Thousand Oaks, Calif.: Sage, 1979.

Cronbach, L. J. *Designing Evaluations of Educational and Social Programs.* San Francisco: Jossey-Bass, 1982.

Datta, L. "Paradigm Wars: A Basis for Peaceful Coexistence and Beyond." In C. S. Reichardt and S. F. Rallis (eds.), *The Qualitative-Quantitative Debate: New Perspectives.* New Directions for Program Evaluation, no. 61. San Francisco: Jossey-Bass, 1994.

DiIulio, J. J., Jr. (ed.). *Deregulating the Public Service: Can Government Be Improved?* Washington, D.C.: The Brookings Institution, 1994.

Gore, A. *From Red Tape to Results: Creating a Government That Works Better and Costs Less.* Washington, D.C.: National Performance Review, 1993.

Greene, J. C., Caracelli, V. J., and Graham, W. F. "Toward a Conceptual Framework for Mixed-Method Evaluation Designs." *Educational Evaluation and Policy Analysis,* 1989, *11* (3), 255–274.

Guba, E. G., and Lincoln, Y. S. *Fourth Generation Evaluation.* Thousand Oaks, Calif.: Sage, 1989.

Hedrick, T. E. "The Quantitative-Qualitative Debate: Possibilities for Integration." In C. S. Reichardt and S. F. Rallis (eds.), *The Qualitative-Quantitative Debate: New Perspectives.* New Directions for Program Evaluation, no. 61. San Francisco: Jossey-Bass, 1994.

Henry, G., Julnes, G. J., and Mark, M. M. (eds.). *Emergent Realist Evaluation.* New Directions for Evaluation, no. 77. San Francisco: Jossey-Bass, in press.

House, E. R. "Realism in Research." *Educational Researcher,* 1991, *20,* 2–9.

House, E. R. "Integrating the Quantitative and the Qualitative." In C. S. Reichardt and S. F. Rallis (eds.), *The Qualitative-Quantitative Debate: New Perspectives.* New Directions for Program Evaluation, no. 61. San Francisco: Jossey-Bass, 1994.

Hudson Institute. *Civil Service 2000.* Indianapolis, Ind.: Hudson Institute, 1988.

Lincoln, Y. S. "The Arts and Sciences of Program Evaluation." *Evaluation Practice,* 1991, *12* (1), 1–7.

Lipsey, M. W. "Theory as Method: Small Theories of Treatments." In L. B. Sechrest and A. G. Scott, *Understanding Causes and Generalizing About Them.* New Directions for Program Evaluation, no. 57. San Francisco: Jossey-Bass, 1993.

Mark, M. M., and Shotland, R. L. "Alternative Models for the Use of Multiple Methods." In M. M. Mark and R. L. Shotland (eds.), *Multiple Methods in Program Evaluation.* New Directions for Program Evaluation, no. 35. San Francisco: Jossey-Bass, 1987.

Mark, M. M., Feller, I., Findeis, J., Musser, W., Shotland, R. L., Stevens, J., Rastegary, H., Button, S., and Vasey, J. *Personnel Management Demonstration Project Final Report.* University Park, Penn.: Institute for Policy Research and Evaluation, 1995.

National Commission on Public Service. *Report and Recommendations of the National Commission on the Public Service.* Washington, D.C.: U.S. Government Printing Office, 1989.

Reichardt, C. S., and Cook, T. D. "Beyond Qualitative *Versus* Quantitative Methods." In T. D. Cook and C. S. Reichardt (eds.), *Qualitative and Quantitative Methods in Evaluation Research.* Thousand Oaks, Calif.: Sage, 1979.

Reichardt, C. S., and Gollob, H. F. "Taking Uncertainty into Account when Estimating Effects." In M. M. Mark and R. L. Shotland (eds.), *Multiple Methods in Program Evaluation.* New Directions for Program Evaluation, no. 35. San Francisco: Jossey-Bass, 1987.

Sechrest, L. "Roots: Back to Our First Generations." *Evaluation Practice,* 1992, *13* (1), 1–7.

Smith, J. K., and Heshusius, L. "Closing down the Conversation: The End of the Quantitative-Qualitative Debate Among Educational Inquirers." *Educational Researcher,* 1986, *15* (1), 4–12.

U.S. Department of Agriculture. "Proposed Demonstration Project." *Federal Register,* 1990, *55* (47), 9062–9076.

U.S. General Accounting Office. *The Changing Workforce: Demographic Issues Facing the Federal Government.* (GAO/GGD–92–38) Washington, D.C.: U.S. General Accounting Office, 1992.

Wholey, J. S. "Evaluability Assessment: Developing Program Theory." In L. Bickman (ed.), *Using Program Theory in Evaluation.* New Directions for Program Evaluation, no. 33. San Francisco: Jossey-Bass, 1987.

MELVIN M. MARK *is professor of psychology at Penn State. He is coeditor (with Gary Henry and George Julnes) of an upcoming issue of* New Directions for Evaluation *on emergent realism, and coauthor (with Chip Reichardt) of a forthcoming volume on quasi-experimentation.*

IRWIN FELLER *is professor of economics and director of the Institute for Policy Research and Evaluation at The Pennsylvania State University. He is active in the evaluation of technology transfer programs.*

SCOTT B. BUTTON *has recently completed his doctorate in industrial/organizational psychology at The Pennsylvania State University. His research interests include work motivation and workforce diversity.*

*The application of mixed methods under the framework of theory-driven evaluations can minimize the potential tension and conflict of mixing qualitative and quantitative methods, as well as compensate for each method's weaknesses. Mixed methods should not be applied indiscriminantly, however, but rather contingently under particular conditions as described in this chapter.*

# Applying Mixed Methods Under the Framework of Theory-Driven Evaluations

*Huey-tsyh Chen*

## Advocating Mixed Methods: A Dominant Methodology for the Future?

There has been a long and emotional debate regarding the best methodology for program evaluation (see Reichardt and Rallis, 1994). Traditionally, quantitative methods have dominated the field of program evaluation. Qualitative methods have also become popular since the late 1970s. Many advocates of qualitative methods have argued forcefully that they should replace quantitative methods as a new dominant methodology (for example, Guba and Lincoln, 1989). This view has been strongly opposed by the quantitative camp (for example, Sechrest, 1992). In addition to this intensive debate, there have recently been a growing number of evaluators advocating for evaluation approaches (for example, Greene, Caracelli, and Graham, 1989) that combine both quantitative and qualitative methods. Because all methods have strengths and weaknesses, advocates of mixed methods argue that the combination gives the best of both worlds. Mixed methods can compensate for method weaknesses, triangulate the evaluative evidence, and expand the scope of study, among other benefits. Due to the attractiveness of mixed methods, some proponents (for example, Datta, 1994) have argued that these methods should constitute the dominant methodology for the future.

From a theory-driven evaluation perspective (Chen, 1990), mixed-method approaches are viewed as useful, but are not seen as a future dominant methodology for both theoretical and practical reasons. Chen (1994) questions the idea that one social inquiry methodology—quantitative, qualitative, or mixed—is likely to replace all others. Past expansion of research methodology has followed a widening path created by increasing numbers of strategies and techniques within each method tradition, rather than one tradition actually replacing another. Quantitative methods and qualitative methods have each made progress on their own criteria and merits. It has rarely been observed that the development of qualitative methods has replaced the functions of quantitative methods, or vice versa. Conceivably, then, mixed methods also have their own merits and can expand our options for evaluation design and data collection, but are unlikely to replace other methods.

In addition, there are four substantive reasons for proponents of theory-driven evaluations to oppose advocating mixed methods as a new dominant methodology.

1. To promote mixed methods as a new dominant methodology implies that mixed methods are superior to other methods. This position would be a burden rather than a blessing for the development of mixed methods, because many contexts are poorly suited to mixed methods. For example, in an evaluation context constrained by time and resources, it is very difficult for mixed methods to compete with quantitative methods in achieving internal validity or with qualitative methods in achieving emic meaning.

2. Program evaluation must deal with many important theoretical and conceptual issues in addition to methodological issues (Chen, 1990). To advocate mixed methods or any other approach as a new dominant methodology might lead to a false hope that mixed methods can solve many of the difficulties and problems in program evaluation. Such advocacy may reinforce the myth that major evaluation problems stem from faulty inquiry methods rather than from insufficient understanding of assumptions and mechanisms underlying a program; this advocacy would sustain the misconception that improving the inquiry method is the key to enhancing the quality of the evaluation.

3. Mixed methods, as will be demonstrated in this chapter, have their own problems and limitations. To advocate mixed methods as a new dominant methodology may hinder evaluators' ability to recognize these problems and develop strategies to address them.

4. The community of program evaluation has already been severely divided by the wars between the quantitative and qualitative camps. To advocate mixed methods as a new dominant methodology may further inflame the methodological wars. Some participants in these wars (for example, Guba and Lincoln, 1989) have already challenged the feasibility and meaningfulness of mixed methods that try to integrate diverse research traditions with opposing views and assumptions about social phenomena. To promote mixed methods as a superior approach, therefore, may only expand the wars that have severely divided the evaluation community by opening another front of conflict.

## The Contingency View for Selecting Mixed Methods and Other Methods

The theory-driven evaluation perspective proposes a contingency approach toward selecting inquiry methods. This approach is based on the premise that no one inquiry method best serves all evaluation needs (Chen, 1990, 1994). Rather, a method's usefulness depends on the contextual circumstances surrounding the specific program to be evaluated. One of the crucial tasks under this approach is, therefore, to identify the contextual circumstances that are most relevant to selecting and applying a particular inquiry method in a given evaluation setting. Some of these contextual circumstances can be conceptualized as the following three dimensions.

1. *The evaluation may be required to produce intensive and contextual versus extensive and precise information.* In some situations, the evaluation may be required to provide an intensive and contextual understanding of program events and activities. For example, stakeholders may need to know in depth why a particular treatment or intervention was chosen, how the client's eligibility was determined, the variety of channels that were used to reach clients, how the program implementors were recruited, and the feelings that both the implementors and clients had about the program experience. The purpose of this kind of inquiry is to provide a holistic picture of the program. On the other hand, an evaluation may be required to provide extensive and precise estimates of the prevalence or incidence of various program elements, or the relationships between them. For example, stakeholders may need to know clients' social and demographic profiles, the number of clients who actually utilize program services, the percentages of clients who were recruited from each channel, and the impact of a treatment on an outcome after one holds all other influences as constant. An evaluation may also be required to provide both types of information.

2. *There may be high availability or accessibility or there may be low availability or accessibility of credible data.* On the one hand, credible data on outcome indicators related to a program, such as birthrates, crime rates, highway incidents, dropout rates, and so forth, can be easily obtained from public records. Other programs may have few outcome measures available in the public records, but evaluators are granted permission to access the target group itself for data collection. This type of data is said to have high availability or accessibility. On the other hand, evaluators may face a situation in which there is low availability or accessibility of credible data related to a program; program implementors may not trust "outsiders" such as evaluators to access the data of the program, or clients may be unwilling to reveal their feelings about the program experience to the evaluator. There may also be situations where some credible data are readily available but other important data are not.

3. *There may be low openness or high openness of environmental influence on a program.* The possibilities range from no influence to continuous influence, or from a completely closed to a completely open system. At one end, an

action program can have low openness and little interaction with its environment. An example of a totally closed system is a laboratory experiment in which a researcher studies a drug's effects on certain animals. Under such conditions, the researcher has full control of the research subjects and research conditions and thereby can manipulate the treatment level and tightly control for confounding influences. At the other end of the dimension, an action program may have high openness with continual interchanges with its environment such that the program is fluid and constantly changing. Program staff members need to react and readjust continually to the environmental influences in order to keep the program alive. Under these conditions, with so many things happening simultaneously, it is highly difficult for evaluators to control the inquiry conditions or perform reliable measurements. Alternatively, an action program may have the characteristics of both an open and a closed system (Chen, 1990). This type of program interacts with its environment in order to acquire resources for survival, but maintains a closed operational core in order to smooth service delivery.

Different program evaluation contexts may have different configurations of these dimensions. Often, factors of these dimensions tend to group into the three configurations shown in Figure 5.1.

Configuration I: This configuration, illustrated in the left-hand side of the figure, indicates those program evaluation contexts that require information to be intensive, have low availability of credible information, and have a highly open program system.

Configuration II: This configuration, illustrated in the right-hand side of Figure 5.1, consists of those program evaluation contexts that require extensive and precise information, have high availability of credible information, and have a closed program system.

Configuration III: The middle illustration of Figure 5.1 indicates a program evaluation context requiring information that is both intensive and extensive, offers high access to some information but low access to other information, and has the characteristics of both open and closed systems.

These patterns suggest the following principles for selecting methods in an evaluation.

1. When an evaluation context's configuration resembles that in Configuration I (requiring intensive and contextual information, offering low availability or accessibility of credible data, and presenting high openness of the system), it is more appropriate to use qualitative methods.

2. When an evaluation context requires extensive and precise information, offers high availability or accessibility of credible data, and presents low openness of the system, as described in Configuration II, quantitative methods are the most appropriate choice.

3. When an evaluation context most resembles that described in Configuration III (requiring both intensive and extensive information, offering only par-

**Figure 5.1. Program Configurations and Choice of Methods**

| Program Configuration I | Program Configuration II | Program Configuration III |
|---|---|---|
| Information is required to be intensive and contextual | | Information is required to be extensive and precise |
| Low availability of credible data | | High availability of credible data |
| Openness in system is high | | Openness in system is low |

| Favoring qualitative methods | Favoring mixed methods | Favoring quantitative methods |
|---|---|---|

tial availability or accessibility of credible data, and presenting characteristics of both open and closed systems), it is more appropriate to use mixed methods.

In this framework, the advocacy of mixed methods would not deny the value of the other methods, which reduces the conflict with advocates of other methods. Instead of asserting that one method is philosophically or ideologically superior to others, the framework suggests that there is room for all methods to coexist in program evaluation, and for all to contribute to the accumulation of evaluation knowledge. This framework challenges the advocates of each method to develop systematic strategies and empirical demonstrations of how their method is useful in particular contexts.

## Mixed Methods Under the Theory-Driven Evaluation Framework

Strategies for evaluating Configuration I, II, or III programs under the framework of theory-driven evaluations have been discussed in Chen (1990). The rest of this chapter attempts to expand Chen's efforts by elaborating on the process of applying mixed methods when evaluating programs resembling Configuration III. One major obstacle for applying mixed methods is that quantitative and qualitative methods are based on contrasting assumptions and ideologies about social phenomena and social knowledge. There are potential tensions and conflicts for using them together in an evaluation. However, under the framework of theory-driven evaluation, these tensions and conflicts are minimized for the following four reasons.

1. *Theory-driven evaluation creates a superordinate goal.* Program theory is the substantive area of focus in the theory-driven evaluation perspective. This substantive focus serves as a superordinate goal for quantitative and qualitative methods to pursue jointly. Pressures are imposed on both types of methods to work together to attain the superordinate goal, rather than to compete or conflict with each other. The demands on evaluation methods under this framework are more concerned with how different methods could be used to understand the nature of program theory and how program theory actually operates, and are less concerned with methodological elegance, purity, or loyalty.

2. *Theory-driven evaluation provides a comprehensive framework for applying component mixed-method designs.* A component mixed-method design refers to combining both quantitative and qualitative methods in a study without altering their original structure. (As discussed in Chapter Two, the combining in such designs occurs at the level of conclusion, leaving each method intact during the inquiry process.) Program theory covers many crucial dimensions and domains of a program, such as treatment (or intervention), goals, implementation system, and environment, as well as the interrelationships between these domains and dimensions. The conceptual framework generated as the program theory provides a comprehensive agenda for applying the component mixed-method design by assigning quantitative and qualitative methods to gather different types or levels of data or to evaluate different portions of a program. For example, qualitative methods can be applied to understand program stakeholders' views and concerns in formulating these domains and dimensions, while quantitative methods can be used to assess relationships between them.

3. *Theory-driven evaluation provides a basis for constructing and applying the integrated mixed-method design.* An integrated mixed-method design (see Chapter Two) synthesizes quantitative and qualitative methods and actually alters the structure of the original methods by creating a different design, which yields evaluation results not possible with either method alone. Method structure can be altered by only partially implementing a method, by preselecting some critical features of a method, or by challenging in some other way the method's traditional integrity. For example, a longitudinal study could combine selected features of both case studies and time series designs for a comprehensive assessment of the interconnections of context and consequences of treatment implementation.

4. *Theory-driven evaluation provides a justification for applying mixed methods.* Evaluation often has to meet multiple purposes or to deal with trade-offs between multiple options such as internal versus external validity (Chen, 1990). According to theory-driven evaluation, one cannot meet such multifaceted evaluation needs easily by using a single method, but can achieve them with component or integrated designs that break down traditional methodological boundaries and selectively integrate elements of quantitative and qualitative methods in design implementation and in results analysis and inferencing.

## Examples of Applying Mixed Methods in Theory-Driven Evaluations

Two recent evaluations that I performed in Taiwan provide concrete examples of applying mixed methods under the framework of theory-driven evaluations.

**Garbage-Reduction Program.** Household garbage in Taiwan has customarily been collected by government sanitation workers on a daily basis. In order to deal with the ever-increasing amount of domestic garbage, the Environmental Protection Agency in Taiwan established a demonstration program that would reduce the amount of domestic garbage that each household generated. The intervention strategy was to enforce a policy of "no garbage dumping or collection each Tuesday." Because the program was a demonstration program, the evaluation results needed to be credible and generalizable. Some of the data, such as daily garbage amounts in the community, were available in the records, but other information, such as data relating to program implementation, was not readily available. This context was a Configuration III type of program.

The funding agency also stressed the need to assess both the effectiveness of the program outcomes and implementation in order to provide concrete information for program improvement (Chen, 1997). This required that evaluators work with program designers to develop both a normative theory and a causative theory of the program (Chen, 1990). The normative theory prescribes what must be done to achieve the desirable goals, while the causative theory specifies why the program is supposed to be effective. According to the normative theory, residents were supposed to be informed about the new policy through letters, banners about the program that were displayed in major streets, and media campaigns. In the implementation stage, sanitation workers were supposed to enforce the "no garbage on Tuesday" policy seriously. Qualitative methods were the most useful tools for determining how residents were actually informed and for observing whether sanitation workers were actually grading the disposal sites and preventing garbage dumping on Tuesdays. For the causative theory, quantitative methods such as surveys and statistical models were most useful for dealing with prevalence issues, such as the extent of resident reaction to the policy, and for precisely assessing the program's effectiveness in reducing the volume of garbage.

The data from the process evaluation indicated that the implemented program closely followed the normative theory. When one applied the multiple time series design, however, the outcome evaluation indicated that the program failed to reduce the volume of domestic garbage. The reason is that the data did not support one aspect of the causative theory. This theory assumed that residents living in apartment housing or small houses with no garage or yard would suffer from the inconvenience and unpleasant smells that having extra garbage in their homes would cause. These negative feelings would remind residents that the garbage problem is serious and that it is important for them to reduce the amount of garbage. However, the data from the survey indicated that the residents did not feel the inconvenience of keeping the garbage in their homes on Tuesdays. Nor did they suffer from the odor of leftover food, because they tied these items in plastic bags with zippers or rubber bands.

This evaluation is an illustration of a component mixed-method design in which different methods were used for different program theory domains and evaluation questions. The program theory underlying the garbage-reduction program served as a superordinate framework for differentially assigning quantitative and qualitative methods to different theory domains. In this case, the two methods complemented one another without tension or conflict.

**Anti–Drug Abuse Program.** Since 1993, the Ministry of Taiwan has implemented an anti–drug abuse program to reduce the use of drugs in the middle schools. The program was developed by a small group of top officials in the Ministry of Education and implemented by administrators and teachers in local schools. The evaluation context resembled that of Configuration III. Some data relating to program operations were available in quarterly reports, but much of the relevant information needed to be gathered from the local schools, which were reluctant to reveal this information to outsiders. The funding agency required the evaluation to be both credible and generalizable.

A normative evaluation under the framework of theory-driven evaluations was selected for the program evaluation (Chen, in press). The major thrust of the normative evaluation was to assess the congruence between the program as specified in the normative theory and the program as it was actually implemented. Evaluators relied on qualitative methods, such as intensive interviews with program designers and local implementors, to develop their normative theory of the program. The normative theory, then, provided a framework for selecting quantitative and qualitative methods to collect data on how the program was actually implemented in the field.

The funding agency requirements for the evaluation to be credible and generalizable were difficult to meet because the school administrators and teachers were skeptical about the evaluation, and because limited time and resources were available for the evaluation. In order to relieve this skepticism, the evaluation team personally visited each school in the sample to assure the administrators and teachers of the confidentiality of the data and to win their support for providing credible data. The visit and data collection for each school were short, however—only one day—so that the team could use the limited resources to visit more schools and thereby increase the sample size and enhance the generalizability of the evaluation findings. The rationale for and implications of constructing such an integrated mixed-method design will be discussed in the next section of this chapter.

The normative theory consisted of crucial domains and dimensions of the program, such as treatment, goals, target group, implementors, mode of delivery, implementing organization, interorganizational linkage, microcontext, and macrocontext. A comprehensive assessment of how the normative theory was operating in the field required that each program theory dimension be assessed with data collected from both quantitative and qualitative methods. For example, within the implementor dimension, quantitative methods were applied to examine the level and prevalence of teacher satisfaction with the Ministry of Education–sponsored workshop on drug abuse counseling skills. Qualitative methods were used to probe teachers' contextual reasons for their reactions to the workshop.

A comparison between the program's normative theory and the program's actual implementation revealed considerable discrepancies. Some of these discrepancies were attributed to the teachers' lack of appropriate training in drug abuse counseling skills and a sense of mistrust and lack of communication between the Ministry of Education and the local schools. This study provides a good illustration of an integrated mixed-method design applied under the theory-driven evaluation framework—a design that met the evaluation's multiple and conflicting needs. Integrated mixed-method designs are not without their problems, however. This point will be expanded in the discussion that follows.

## Some Strengths and Weaknesses of Mixed Methods

One of the major strengths of mixed methods is that evaluators can flexibly use or tailor quantitative and qualitative methods to meet evaluation needs. Mixed methods are particularly useful when the evaluation needs to meet multiple requirements or deal with trade-offs. The evaluation of the anti–drug abuse program illustrates this point well. As mentioned earlier, the funding agency required the evaluation to be both credible and generalizable. There were 734 middle schools in Taiwan. The evaluators could have rigorously applied a quantitative method, such as drawing a large random sample for a mail survey or telephone interview, in order to ensure the generalizability of the evaluation. However, due to school administrators' and teachers' high skepticism about the evaluation, mail surveys or telephone interviews would probably have yielded superficial, misleading, and incomplete data that would not have been credible. Alternatively, the evaluators could have taken a strong qualitative approach and selected a few schools for intensive case studies. This application would have produced in-depth and trustworthy data regarding program implementation, but would not have met the requirements for generalizability.

To handle this dilemma, the evaluation design blended selected quantitative and qualitative methods to produce an integrated mixed-method design. The integrated design consisted of a one-day visit and data collection for each school in the evaluation team's sample. The personal visit and assurance of confidentiality enhanced administrators' and teachers' trust and cooperation in providing credible data. The short visit allowed the team to save resources for a larger sample size in order to enhance generalizability. The resources of the evaluation allowed the team to include thirty-one schools in the sample for the study. The selection of the thirty-one schools benefited from the wisdom of quantitative methods. In order to increase the sample's representativeness, the team stratified schools according to regimes and school size. The evaluators then randomly drew the sample from these strata. This mixed-method sample design and data collection enabled this evaluation to meet the require-ments of both credibility and generalizability more adequately than could a single-method design.

The flexibility of mixed methods is not without its costs, however, notably with respect to methodological rigor. In a single-method evaluation, the eval-uator needs to be concerned with only one kind of rigor, representing either a qualitative or a quantitative tradition. However, a mixed-method evaluation needs to meet standards of rigor for both quantitative and qualitative methods. This may not be a problem if the evaluator has sufficient resources and time to pursue standards of dual rigor. More often, however, applying mixed methods requires the evaluator to divide limited resources between the quantitative and qualitative components in an evaluation. Because of this division of resources, it is understandable that the rigor of the mixed methods may be compromised in comparison with a single-method evaluation. This risk to rigor may be even higher in an integrated mixed-method design than a component mixed-method design. Because the integrated design requires structural changes in the methods themselves, traditional standards of quantitative and qualitative quality and rigor may become harder to meet in integrated designs.

These challenges to rigor are indeed problematic when mixed methods are applied under the framework of method-driven evaluations. Since meth-ods are the infrastructure of method-driven evaluations, compromised rigor in mixed-method designs can directly undermine the soundness and strength of their inferences. However, the lower rigor may not necessarily lead to a weakened inference when mixed methods are applied under the framework of theory-driven evaluations. The strength of inferences in a theory-driven evaluation comes from both methodological rigor and theoretical reasoning.

For example, a one-day visit is far from sufficient to generate a thick description according to the qualitative tradition. However, in-depth knowl-edge of the program's normative theory allowed evaluators to cut short the length of stay in each school and still collect the essential data about imple-mentation. Similarly, a sample size of 31 out of 734 schools is too small to be representative, according to quantitative standards. As Chen (1990) points out, however, generalizability can be achieved through statistical approaches (for example, a representative sample) or theoretical approaches (for example, the-oretical knowledge of the research and generalizing system). In the anti–drug abuse study, the intensive knowledge of the theoretical domains and dimen-sions of implementation, such as treatment, goals, implementors, implement-ing organizations, and interorganizational linkage, allowed the evaluators to make a strong argument that the schools not included in the sample operated under the same education system and faced similar problems, and would therefore show similar patterns concerning the program's implementation.

Another strategy used in theory-driven evaluation to strengthen reason-ing, or to compensate for the risk to rigor when mixed methods are applied, is to use the linked and nested data to reinforce the evaluation findings or to resolve inconsistencies in the data. Data collected under the framework of theory-driven evaluation are theoretically nested and linked. For example, the data in a dimension (for example, the implementor dimension) are either linked with the data in another dimension (such as the delivery mode dimension) or nested under a broad domain (for example, the implementation domain). Considering the evaluation of the anti–drug abuse program, data that indicated that the counseling sessions were not adequate for the students were reinforced by data that indicated that the teachers were not properly trained in counseling skills. This is a case in which linked data are used to support the findings in each domain. Furthermore, if the data appear to be inconsistent in one area, evaluators can use the contextual information to reconcile the inconsistencies. If we use the garbage-reduction program as an example, the data indicated that the program was properly implemented but ineffective in reducing the volume of garbage. This inconsistency is reconciled if we include the fact that residents neither felt inconvenience in storing garbage at home on Tuesday nor smelled its unpleasant odor. One crucial chain in the underlying causal mechanisms failed to operate appropriately. Chen (1990) discusses other theoretical strategies for strengthening reasoning, such as pattern matching and investigation of rival hypotheses.

## Conclusions

From a contingency point of view, the theory-driven evaluation perspective argues that mixed methods are neither superior to other methods in every circumstance nor applicable in every evaluation situation. When applied appropriately, however, such as in an evaluation context resembling a Configuration III type of program or when the evaluation includes multiple and conflicting requirements, mixed methods can provide highly insightful and useful information for the evaluation. This chapter also indicated that it is important to understand the potential problems and limitations that mixed methods can bring. Since mixed methods often require evaluators to divide limited resources between quantitative and qualitative methods, the rigor of each method is likely to be compromised. However, these challenges to rigor are mitigated when mixed methods are applied under the framework of the theory-driven evaluation. In such an application, methodological considerations can be integrated with theoretical strategies to enhance the strength of inferences in the evaluation.

## References

Chen, H.-T. *Theory-Driven Evaluations.* Thousand Oaks, Calif.: Sage, 1990.

Chen, H.-T. "Current Trends and Future Directions in Program Evaluation." *Evaluation Practice,* 1994, *15* (3), 229–238.

Chen, H.-T. "Evaluating the Process and Outcome of a Garbage Reduction Program in Taiwan." *Evaluation Review,* 1997, *21* (1), 27–42.

Chen, H.-T. "Normative Evaluation of an Anti–Drug Abuse Program." *Evaluation and Program Planning,* in press.

Datta, L. "Paradigm Wars: A Basis for Peaceful Coexistence and Beyond." In C. S. Reichardt and S. F. Rallis (eds.), *The Qualitative-Quantitative Debate: New Perspectives.* New Directions for Program Evaluation, no. 61. San Francisco: Jossey-Bass, 1994.

Greene, J. C., Caracelli, V. J., and Graham, W. F. "Toward a Conceptual Framework for Mixed-Method Evaluation Designs." *Educational Evaluation and Policy Analysis,* 1989, *11* (3), 255–274.

Guba, E. G., and Lincoln, Y. S. *Fourth Generation Evaluation.* Thousand Oaks, Calif.: Sage, 1989.

Reichardt, C. S., and Rallis, S. F. (eds.). *The Qualitative-Quantitative Debate: New Perspectives.* New Directions for Program Evaluation, no. 61. San Francisco: Jossey-Bass, 1994.

Sechrest, L. "Roots: Back to Our First Generations." *Evaluation Practice,* 1992, *13* (1), 1–7.

*HUEY-TSYH CHEN is professor of sociology at the University of Akron. He received the American Evaluation Association's Lazarsfeld Award of Evaluation Theory in 1993.*

*To extend the conversation on mixing methods, we must look less at formal paradigms and more at the crude mental models and cases of evaluation practice.*

# Mixing and Matching: Methods and Models

*Mary Lee Smith*

The evaluation literature is famous for its debates over the compatibility of paradigms and methods. Some methodologists lean toward the idea that methods belong to philosophical systems. Others see no such link and argue for more practical considerations—that is, using qualitative and quantitative methods to address different kinds of questions. (In Chapter One of this volume, Greene and Caracelli refer to these types of people respectively as purists and pragmatists.) Although calls for rapprochement are persuasive, the debate is far from settled.

I believe that the explanation for this gap lies in the power of crude models or metaphors that exist in the minds of evaluators and guide their actions. It is a useful principle of symbolic interactionism (for example, Blumer, 1969) that action is impossible unless one has constructed a mental model, image, or definition of the situation. This claim pertains to the act of inquiry no less than to any other social action. A particular evaluation rests on the evaluator's mental picture of what the world is like, how evaluations ought to be, and what counts as knowledge. Because evaluation is social action, an act of inquiry rests also on expectations of what standards the relevant community will likely apply to it.

Phillips (1996) expanded this notion of mental models, which he associated with "assumptions, analogies, metaphors, or crude models that are held at the very outset of the researcher's work . . . [and] are present even before any [formal] theories or [explicit] models have been constructed" (pp. 1008–1009). It is important to distinguish these crude presumptive models from paradigms (Greene and Caracelli, Chapter One of this volume), although the two may coincide in some evaluators. If we want to understand the nature of

New Directions for Evaluation, no. 74, Summer 1997 © Jossey-Bass Publishers

mixed-method evaluations, we must look not at paradigms but at the crude model that activates particular evaluations. Looking at paradigms has distracted and distorted the "conversation" that motivates the present volume.

Paradigms are formal philosophical systems, born and nurtured in the armchair. They are abstract, generalized, and logically consistent. From the paradigm vantage point, it is sensible to argue about commensurability or about the death of positivism. Actual evaluations take place in more complicated and messy arenas—in real times and places, conducted by particular individuals and groups. Initial designs, as well as the day-to-day decisions, negotiations, and compromises that seem to characterize all inquiry projects, depend on the crude mental models of the people involved.

A paradigm is a formal philosophical system and as such is bound by logic and inner consistency. The crude model, on the other hand, is peculiar to an individual or shared within a face-to-face group and emerges from disciplinary, cultural, historical, social, and ideological roots. It is the crude model that gauges the potential meaning and usefulness of employing Method A or Method B or some combination of A and B. Likewise, it is the crude model that embeds standards for considering the information yield of these methods. Abstract arguments about commensurability and compatibility break down when the evaluator asks (consciously or unconsciously), What knowledge can we extract from this inquiry, and on what criteria should these inferences be judged?

To extend the conversation about mixed methods, therefore, one must deemphasize questions about general paradigms and think more about crude models in particular cases. It is not so much a matter of asking, for example, What are the tenets of logical positivism, and are they consistent with one or another research procedure? Rather, ascertaining one's mental model amounts to shaking an evaluator awake in the middle of the night and asking, Is it possible to have validity without reliability? Or, Can an evaluator know anything about a program without having seen it in action personally? The responses to these middle-of-the-night questions characterize the mental models I exemplify in the following paragraphs, and they relate to the use of mixed methods in evaluations.

## A Few Mental Models and the "Method-Mixing" Practices That Follow from Them

Three mental models are described through an interplay of reflections on practical experience and conceptual reasoning.

**Mental Model I.** Some colleagues of mine who do very good work developing secondary prevention programs for children at psychological risk wanted help in adding qualitative components to their evaluation studies. They had a vague sense that something was missing from their usual experimental designs and psychometric measures of risk. On my advice, they hired several graduate students to serve as a qualitative team to conduct clinical interviews with participants and observe therapy groups.

From these data, the qualitative team developed some themes about problematic interactions within groups that may have impeded the program's effectiveness. The psychologists' reactions to the results of the qualitative data analysis were troublesome, because their images of what counts as evaluation did not fit with what the qualitative data were able to provide. Some found the data intriguing, but not significant. They believed that without the trappings of experimental procedures, including interobserver agreement rates, the data were unconvincing and unpublishable in their usual journals. Others resented that resources had been needlessly siphoned away from the quantitative analysis and dismissed the analysis outright.

I refer to the set of presumptions and mental pictures these psychologist-evaluators hold as Model I. They believe there is a single reality separate from individuals' interpretations of it, and that definitive knowledge is possible. They believe that the more precise the measures and the more controlled the design, the stronger the inferences are that can be drawn from them. Trustworthy inferences are those that are "mechanized" (Behrens and Smith, 1996), based on the straightforward testing of null hypotheses. The standards that they apply and that they expect their community to apply to the results are reliability, reproducibility, internal validity, and cross-context generalization.

With such a mental model of what good evaluation is, what role could data from participant observation possibly play? Very likely, these data would be reduced to the role of "thin description" (Geertz, 1973). At most, they would provide a little color or human interest but would certainly not contribute to making inferences. If the impressions formed from the qualitative data conflicted with the inferences from the quantitative data, the former would likely be discounted because they cannot meet the standards of reliability and reproducibility, much less validity. To the extent that a particular evaluator holds such views of the world and of what constitutes appropriate inquiry, incorporating qualitative methods makes little sense.

**Mental Model II.** Model II is slightly more nuanced and compatible with combining methods than is Model I. Those who hold Model II presume a real world that is beyond the interpretations of any individual, but also one that cannot be studied free of individual perspective. They understand that each method of study has a characteristic weakness, and that each perspective is partial and biased in some way. Dependable knowledge is possible, however, if the results of independent accounts based on multiple methods converge. Dependable inferences can be made from the extent of the convergence.

What does mixed-method evaluation look like from this model of viewing the world? The qualitative and quantitative components must be conducted separately and simultaneously. Otherwise, the sources of error and bias would not be independent. Designs that allowed the components to inform one another mutually or that were sequential ("complementarity" and "development" designs in the Greene, Caracelli, and Graham, 1989, typology) would violate the criterion of independence. My attempts to mix methods would have failed this standard of independence. For example, in our study of practices of identifying learning disabilities (Shepard, Smith, and Vojir, 1983), Lorrie Shepard and I were in constant contact, and our conceptions of how to frame the questions and interpret the data in, respectively, the quantitative and qualitative components were mutually informed. To conform to Model II, however, the components must be independent of each other. Inferences can be drawn from the extent to which the findings of the separate and independent components corroborate each other.

Furthermore, the study questions, units, and variables of the components would have to be equivalent. The triangulation design that follows from Model II would have both components aiming to generate similar kinds of inferences (that is, a psychometric measure of children's adjustment compared with a clinician's coding of adjustment from open-ended interviews with the children). If, on the other hand, the quantitative component addressed the effects of therapy groups on the participants' psychological adjustment while the qualitative component addressed the emotionality of interaction within the groups, there would be no area of possible convergence across the findings of the components. Triangulation in Model II assumes that there is a reality to triangulate *on,* as Mathison (1988) noted. Thus, the evaluation design follows from a belief, for example, that the reduction of psychological risk as a result of a secondary prevention program is a real thing, and that reliable and intersubjective knowledge can be gained from it. Someone holding a model such as this would tend to mix methods, but in perhaps a restrictive way, believing that the complexities of the world can and should be resolved into a single definitive value.

**Mental Model III.** The world assumed in Model III is complex, contextually contingent, and mediated by individual interpretations of it. A definitive account of the phenomenon of interest is not possible, although accounts based on extensive, intensive, and comprehensive views can be better than others. Analysis is based on the inquirer's recognition of patterns of meaning and social action, followed by a systematic and self-critical process of asking, Is this a pattern or merely noise? Have I named it properly? What other elements and patterns explain it? Does my explanation stand up against competing evidence and explanations? The analysis contributes to "thick description," in other words, description intended to contribute to contextual and theoretical understanding (Geertz, 1973).

Because the analysis is the construction of the inquirer, she is free to learn from components that focus on different questions, units, and variables. The emotionality of social interaction in therapy groups observed qualitatively would be as relevant as quantitative measures of psychological adjustment in the inquirer's aim to understand and value the secondary prevention programs for at-risk children. Contextualized social processes are just as important to explain as structural variables are, as Maxwell (1996) argued and as Cronbach (1982) demonstrated in the INCAP study. If one looks at reality as being complex and social, it is important to try to explain the unfolding social action in a program, a therapy group, or a classroom. Qualitative and narrative techniques are especially able to build explanations about social process. To get close enough to the process to describe and interpret it appropriately requires the inquirer to participate in it to some degree. (The attendant loss of detachment and "objectivity" may be too much for some evaluators to bear, and certainly reduces the possibility for reproducibility and interobserver agreement.)

Qualitative knowing is at the heart of Model III. Quantitative techniques can also be informative, however, once the inquirer recognizes the patterns in the data (Erickson, 1986, calls this counting in context). From data in the form of numbers, one makes inferences in the same way as with data in the form of words, not by virtue of probabilistic algorithms. Statistics are not privileged. Inference is not mechanized. With this way of viewing knowledge, "mixed" methods may even be a misnomer, as both surveys and participant observations yield equivalent data (Behrens and Smith, 1996). Inferences are based on the inquirer's coordinating multiple lines of evidence to gain an overall understanding of the phenomenon. One uses several methods because each provides a different perspective on the phenomenon. Each method has fallibilities and is based on particular assumptions, therefore a single method limits one's understandings. Yet, because the inquirer is the instrument, all information flows through a single perspective.

Standards for judging inferences are embedded in the model. Although the possibilities for reproducibility and reliability are lost to the need for close-up inspection and participation, the inquirer still worries about appropriate relationships with participants as a means of accessing relevant data, and about precision, rigor, and comprehensiveness (scope and time) of data collection. These are time-honored norms of fieldwork, as argued specifically in Erickson (1986).

The view of the world as complex and socially constructed is consistent with a standard for narrative adequacy, verisimilitude, fidelity, and thick description (Blumenfeld-Jones, 1995; Denzin, 1989; Eisner, 1991). Convergence across methods is not a standard of validity, as it is in Model II, and the inquirer does not necessarily expect it (Mathison, 1988). Instead, the standard of a valid account rests on establishing coherence across multiple lines of evidence and argument (Eisner, 1991, referred to this as structural corroboration). Erickson (1986) invoked the standards of coherence and plausibility as applied to accounts of this type. The inquirer engages in self-analysis and self-criticism throughout the study and reveals to the reader his or her evolving perspective and enough of the data to allow the reader to participate as a coanalyst.

As Phillips (1996) pointed out, individuals' mental models influence what kinds of questions they judge suitable for study, what approaches they will take, and what standards of truth they will attach to the results. Certainly, the models influence whether or how methods will be combined, and what and how inferences will be drawn from data. Although the three models illustrated are typical, they do not exhaust possible models. I neglected critical, social realist, and postmodern models only because of limited space, not because of relative importance. Having established the connection between mental models and mixing methods, I present a case of mixing methods consistent with Model III.

## A Case of Mixing Methods: Model III

Between 1990 and 1995, the Arizona Student Assessment Program (ASAP) was a state mandate designed to make Arizona public schools accountable to the state's curriculum frameworks, as well as to reform instruction toward thematic, integrated subject matter, higher-order thinking, and problem-solving skills. The program to achieve these goals consisted of: (1) a series of mandated performance-based tests; (2) reporting requirements so that student, school, and district achievement could be made public; and (3) other accountability and certification mechanisms (for example, high school graduation mastery levels on test performance) to be phased in later.

Teaching in ways that promote achievement on performance tests involves learning new forms of pedagogy and requires alternative kinds of texts and materials. This new form of pedagogy is associated with constructivism and contrasts with a behaviorist, basic skills form of pedagogy that dominated the state prior to ASAP. Despite the substantial retraining requirements needed to implement ASAP, the state failed to fund staff or curriculum development. Instead, the policy assumed that teachers and schools would adapt their teaching to the alternative assessment if high stakes were attached to its results. This "Field of Dreams" assumption (Noble and Smith, 1994) is not unlike that of assessment policies of several other states and of the federal assessment policy embodied in *Goals 2000*.

Our study of ASAP was both longitudinal and multifaceted, involving policy analysis, multiple case studies, focus group interviews, and representative surveys of educators. Our aim was to understand educators' responses to this sweeping mandate, in particular how the introduction of ASAP might have influenced curriculum, pedagogy, school organization, and teachers' meanings and actions.

Consistent with our mental models, we presumed that governmental mandates such as ASAP are based on images, values, and intentions that may be harmonious or discordant with local images, values, intentions, and practices. Furthermore, local variations may compromise and alter the features of centrally imposed policy (Combs, 1991). Holding this view of society and policy, we rejected a simple model of causality.

Reducing uncertainty about the effects of ASAP assumed a lower priority than constructing a coherent, credible account of local practitioner and district responses to it. The best way to accomplish this was to establish relationships with a few schools in which we could be firsthand observers over the course of a year to discover how (or whether) educational practices were changing in response to ASAP. Moreover, we wanted to listen to educators as they expressed their reactions to the state program, and understand the processes or sequences of social transactions that might later explain patterns of response. In our effort to capture meaning and action in contexually sensitive narratives, precision of measurement, interobserver reliability, and generalizability were not as important to us as the extensiveness and intensiveness of participant observation.

We used qualitative analysis procedures and constructed case studies and vignettes to depict the first year of ASAP in four schools and to examine the themes and categories that emerged. At the end of the second year of ASAP implementation, we returned to the four schools for another round of interviews. Among other things, our analyses revealed a model of local response. In it, several conditions seemed to influence how educators responded to ASAP. These conditions included the financial resources to fund curriculum and staff development, the availability of a local reform expert to facilitate the necessary modifications, the district's valuing of authority and accountability, and ASAP's compatibility with the dominant local educational ideologies. In other words, local responses coherent with ASAP intentions seemed to occur in places where there was: sufficient district wealth to fund capacity development; the presence of someone at school to interpret ASAP provisions and instruct educators how to teach integrated, thematic, problem-solving pedagogy; low investment in standardized test-based accountability and low test burden; and low investment in behaviorist, basic skills education (as opposed to constructivist pedagogy, with which ASAP was compatible). The data suggested that change toward ASAP intentions was limited to those sites that had been already moving toward constructivist pedagogy independent of and prior to ASAP.

Although our mental model predisposed us toward qualitative approaches, we believed that survey techniques could provide another angle on the program and could possibly allow us to generalize the working hypotheses and patterns that we developed in the case studies to broad and representative samples. We also recognized that some audiences attach greater credence to quantitative data. For the survey component of the study, we constructed questionnaire items that reflected what we had learned from the four school case studies and policy review. For example, a typical selling point that state department officials mentioned to teachers was made into a questionnaire item to which the sample might agree or disagree: "ASAP represents the best we know about how students learn." Tapping the local response model described above, we constructed items such as: "The principal is supportive of integrated, holistic, problem-solving education," and "Many teachers disagree with the philosophy of curriculum, instruction, and assessment that ASAP represents."

We assessed the effects of the program (at least as screened through teachers' interpretations) with items such as the following: "As a result of ASAP, major changes in curriculum have been made at school," and "Adequate professional development has been provided for teachers to make changes necessary to implement ASAP," and "Students have adequate opportunity to learn higher-order thinking skills."

We also provided items that addressed the perceived validity and fairness of the state tests themselves. We used standard survey research methods to develop and pilot test the instruments, select the samples, and analyze the results. Adequate response rates from the probability sample permitted us to generalize the results to the population of teachers and administrators. We computed item-level frequencies, as well as complex regression analyses that addressed such issues as the relationship between pupils' ethnic composition and their response to ASAP. One of the survey's many findings was that positive response to ASAP was highly variable from place to place and low overall. For example, over 50 percent of teachers agreed with the statement, "ASAP has had little or no effect on my teaching."

To complement the data from the survey, we selected several schools and conducted focus group interviews with their teachers. We sampled four schools theoretically to parallel our original cases and test the local response model generated from the multiple case study data. Two schools had participated in an earlier study of the role of state-mandated standardized tests (Smith and others, 1989). A colleague (Parish, 1996) studied two other schools from the same district that had contributed one of our case study sites, and we added her data to ours.

In addition to the new interview data, we paid close attention to the open-ended responses on the questionnaire. Many members of the sample wrote thoughtfully and at length about their reactions to ASAP. We recognized that these data are not representative of the population, but they do not suffer the constraints of the forced choice structure of the questionnaire items. Adding the survey, the focus groups, and the careful review of open-ended questionnaire responses rested on the presumption that all methods have fallibilities and partialities and that robust inferences depend on multiple points of viewing.

Taken together, the components of the study left us with a massive amount of data of such unevenness and apparent dissimilarity that they nearly defied synthesis. Although each component had been analyzed by appropriate methods and reported separately, we felt that the power of the study must lie in the integration of data. We decided to apply Erickson's modified method (1986) of analytic induction as a way to integrate these data.

Although commonly associated with the interpretive qualitative approach, Erickson's method cohered with our aim, our standards, and our viewpoint on the treatment of data. That is, whether data happen to be in the form of words or in the form of numbers should not materially affect the process of constructing meaning from them. Both forms of data are symbolic and neither is inherently "harder" or "softer" than the other. Analysis of both quantitative and qualitative data involves construction and reduction at appropriate times. Even employing analytic algorithms falls short of attaining a definitive solution for either kind of data (Behrens and Smith, 1996). With the ASAP data, we believed that we could adopt the same model, even though some of the data were in the form of statistics.

Erickson's method is based on the researcher's repeated reading of the data as a whole and then arriving inductively and intuitively at a set of credible assertions. Assertions are statements that the researcher believes to be true based on an understanding of all the data. Next, the researcher goes through a process of establishing the warrant for each assertion, assembling the confirming evidence from the record of data, searching vigorously for disconfirming evidence, weighing the evidence one way or the other, and then casting out unwarranted assertions or substantially altering them so they fit with the data. Having settled on a final list of warranted assertions and any linkages between them, the researcher then builds representations of the evidence so that the reader can participate as coanalyst. The reader has access to the full range of evidence in the form of vignettes, synoptic description, interpretative commentary, and a history of the development of the researcher's thinking from conceptualization of the study to final report. The researcher is striving for a credible, coherent report based on evidence adequate in amount and varied in kind and an analysis that proceeds with healthy skepticism and self-criticism.

I began the integrative analysis of the ASAP data by assembling and then reading the data from all parts of the study at least three times. With memos, I kept track of the themes and concepts that arose during this reading. Two working assumptions guided this phase of the work. One was that I could only work with data at their least processed level. In other words, when interview transcripts were available, as was usually true, they became the data to be analyzed. The case study reports themselves were treated as data when the researchers' observation write-ups were not available. Similarly, the descriptive statistics from the survey were treated as data, rather than any inferential statistics, such as regression coefficients, that had been computed during the survey research study. The second working assumption had to do with my orientation toward the different kinds of data. Qualitative and quantitative data were treated as equivalent, neither type privileged over the other in terms of its potential to inform.

From the repeated readings of data (which ran to more than 2,500 pages), I generated a set of preliminary assertions. One such assertion stated: "Unlike many state programs, Arizona teachers seem quite well aware about ASAP, although exactly *how* they understand and define it varies dramatically from person to person, almost as if people were talking about a completely different entity but using the same label." At this early stage, there were a dozen ambiguous and complex sentences like this on the list, and the contents of some overlapped others.

I next began a process of refining and establishing the warrant for each assertion, a process that might be described as the exercise of disciplined skepticism. Erickson (1986) stated that the researcher must look for reasons to hold the work suspect. Warranting proceeds one assertion at a time and involves a systematic search through the data record for segments that support or confirm the assertion. Data segments that support the assertion—such as passages from interview transcripts, observation write-ups, or descriptive statistics from survey responses—then became "instances" or "indicators." I then organized and indexed these pieces of evidence (many analysts appreciate qualitative data analysis packages for this part, but I used low-tech methods such as sticky notes and text markers). I paid particular attention to confirming instances that more than one data collection method generated. This practice follows the assumption that assertions based on a sole form of data (for example, questionnaire responses only or focus group interview only) are less robust and persuasive than assertions based on multiple data sources.

Having identified and catalogued the confirming instances, I then searched for disconfirming instances, the discovery of which provoked rethinking, recasting, or revising of the assertion. If disconfirming evidence had been sufficiently weighty, an assertion would have been discarded outright, but this did not happen. In Erickson's method, there is no acid test or mechanized means for determining the balance of confirming versus disconfirming evidence. Instead, the researcher's reasoned and disciplined weighting of evidence can be supported by peer or participant review; readers judge the plausibility of the account.

In the ASAP study, one preliminary assertion that was subsequently revised based on the weight of evidence had been stated: "Exclusive of the sites that were moving on their own toward constructivism, ASAP has produced little coherent change." Challenging this claim was the evidence Parish (1996) presented on Desert School, where educators had seized on the opportunity ASAP provided to make dramatic and categorical changes in curriculum, teaching methods, assessment, and staff development, even though no constructivist practice had been evident before ASAP. This account persuaded me to rethink my unduly pessimistic interpretation of the evidence. Thereafter, I looked for types of change, rather than a simple "change" or "no change" category, and eventually stated an assertion more consistent with the data (see Exhibit 6.1, Assertion 4).

Part of the warranting process involved looking for negative or discrepant cases that violated the patterns I had found. I had asserted that local conditions—ideologies and images of learning and curriculum, resources, and accountability or authority structures—all had to be working in concert for ASAP to take hold. The data from the last set of focus group interviews challenged that pattern. Interesting changes toward ASAP goals had occurred in a school with a strong accountability culture and anticonstructivist pedagogy. I carefully examined the data from that school and developed the notion of a micropolitical process that undercuts those local structures and has an effect on change toward or away from ASAP ideals.

Following through with the warranting process for each preliminary assertion and sorting through redundancies and overlaps, I eventually arrived at a final list of eight assertions (see Exhibit 6.1). Supporting evidence was sufficiently compelling, diverse, and complete to make me confident in that list. So far, however, the knowledge constructed was solely my own. The next step was to build knowledge representations for potential readers by selecting data excerpts that would best depict the central ideas, themes, and patterns in each assertion. The selection aimed not for statistical generalization but for analytic generalization (Glaser, 1978), that is, to demonstrate an obvious tie between concepts or categories and the referents on which the concepts rest. An example of this process is the category "Drag" that I developed from the data. This referred to the burden that ASAP's many tests and accountability requirements put on schools that were already far along the route toward constructivist education before ASAP came along.

## Exhibit 6.1. Final List of Assertions from Mixed-Method Study

Assertion 1: Most educators were aware of ASAP, although their definitions of "ASAP" varied.

Assertion 2: Approval of ASAP was far from universal.

Assertion 3: Action coherent with policy intents had begun to be realized in some places. Categories of response were: compliance only, compromise, coherent action, drag.

Assertion 4: Responses coherent with ASAP intentions were centered in a few places where circumstances were auspicious.

Assertion 5: Inadequate capacity, as well as capacity building, impeded coherent response to ASAP intentions.

Assertion 6: State inattention to the technical and administrative adequacy of the assessment and accountability system impeded coherent responses to ASAP intentions.

Assertion 7: The reform intention and the accountability intention of ASAP conflicted with each other, and the conflict impeded coherent action.

Assertion 8: The lack of attention at the state level to concerns for equity and fairness inhibited coherent local responses to the policy.

*Source:* Smith, 1996.

To serve the same purpose, I constructed analytic vignettes (Erickson, 1986) to demonstrate the voice of the participants and to portray the social processes that led them to accommodate the program. Both the quoted excerpts and the vignettes demonstrate for the reader the veracity of the assertion and provide concrete particulars in a vivid slice of life. By reading these details, the reader should be able to judge the process by which the researcher arrived at the assertions and gain understanding through vicarious experience. Finally, interpretive commentary linked the assertions and data and pointed to links with extant literature and theory. The full report of the ASAP reform (which the state has since suspended) is available in Smith (1996).

## Comments

Although this was obviously a case of mixing methods, whether this ASAP study involved mixed paradigms begs the question. The preceding description of the ASAP study illustrates well the particular mental model that guided it: the aim (understanding), the view of the world (as complex, contingent, social, with local action and meaning affecting policy as much as they were affected by it), the view of knowledge (as provisional, constructed, producing credibility and coherence rather than proof), and the image of methods (as fallible and rich with bias and assumptions). The importance of the fit between mental model and the project is most clearly revealed in the expectations of appropriate standards (for example, comprehensiveness of view and narrative value rather than internal validity or reliability).

Although the survey component of the ASAP study may have attained the standards and matched the presumptions of Model I, the qualitative data would have lacked reliability, replicability, and internal and external validity. They would have been appropriate only for human interest, but could not have sustained valid inference. Even though we had multiple data collection methods, we could hardly have achieved the standards of valid inference explicit in Model II, for the component studies were anything but independent. At every step of the study, method error and perspective bias spilled from one element to the others. If data from the quantitative and qualitative methods had happened to corroborate each other, this event could have been explained away because a single cognitive framework had coordinated and informed each piece. If the data had diverged, one could have blamed method variance and bias. My claim to the validity of the work lies in the extensiveness of data and the comprehensiveness of views on the phenomenon, on the coherence of assumptions, frameworks, data, and inferences, and on the plausibility of the account.

In summary, models matter. Crude models matter more than formal philosophical systems in explaining how evaluators practice. If one does not understand one's presumptions, predispositions, and expectations about criteria, one's mixing of evaluation procedures is likely to remain problematic.

## References

Behrens, J., and Smith, M. L. "Data and Data Analysis." In D. C. Berliner and R. C. Calfee (eds.), *Handbook of Educational Psychology*. Old Tappan, N.J.: Macmillan, 1996.

Blumenfeld-Jones, D. "Fidelity as a Criterion for Practicing and Evaluating Narrative Inquiry." *International Journal of Qualitative Studies in Education*, 1995, *8* (1), 25–36.

Blumer, H. *Symbolic Interactionism: Perspective and Method*. Berkeley: University of California Press, 1969.

Combs, A. W. *The Schools We Need: New Assumptions for Educational Reform*. Lanham, Md.: University Press of America, 1991.

Cronbach, L. J. *Designing Evaluations of Educational and Social Programs*. San Francisco: Jossey-Bass, 1982.

Denzin, N. K. *Interpretive Interactionism*. Thousand Oaks, Calif.: Sage, 1989.

Eisner, E. *The Enlightened Eye*. Old Tappan, N.J.: Macmillan, 1991.

Erickson, F. E. "Qualitative Methods in Research on Teaching." In M. Wittrock (ed.), *Handbook of Research on Teaching*. (3rd ed.) Old Tappan, N.J.: Macmillan, 1986.

Geertz, C. *Interpretation of Cultures*. New York: Basic Books, 1973.

Glaser, B. G. *Theoretical Sensitivity*. Mill Valley, Calif.: Sociological Press, 1978.

Greene, J. C., Caracelli, V. J., and Graham, W. F. "Toward a Conceptual Framework for Mixed-Method Evaluation Designs." *Educational Evaluation and Policy Analysis*, 1989, *11* (3), 255–274.

Mathison, S. "Why Triangulate?" *Educational Researcher*, 1988, *17* (2), 13–17.

Maxwell, J. A. *Qualitative Research Design: An Interactive Approach*. Applied Social Research Methods Series, no. 41. Thousand Oaks, Calif.: Sage, 1996.

Noble, A. J., and Smith, M. L. "Old and New Beliefs About Measurement-Driven Reform: 'Build It and They Will Come.'" *Educational Policy*, 1994, *8* (2), 111–136.

Parish, C. A. "Changes in Practice Accompanying the Implementation of the Arizona Student Assessment Plan." Unpublished doctoral dissertation, College of Education, Educational Leadership and Policy Studies, Arizona State University-Tempe, 1996.

Phillips, D. C. "Philosophical Perspectives." In D. C. Berliner and R. C. Calfee (eds.), *Handbook of Educational Psychology*. Old Tappan, N.J.: Macmillan, 1996.

Shepard, L. A., Smith, M. L., and Vojir, C. "Characteristics of Pupils Identified as Learning Disabled." *American Educational Research Journal*, 1983, *20*, 309–332.

Smith, M. L. *Reforming Schools by Reforming Assessment: Consequences of the Arizona Student Assessment Program.* Los Angeles: Center for the Study of Evaluation/Center for Research on Educational Standards and Student Testing, University of California, 1996.

Smith, M. L., Edelsky, C., Draper, K., Rottenberg, C., and Cherland, M. *The Role of Testing in Elementary Schools.* Technical report no. 321. Los Angeles: Center for the Study of Evaluation/Center for Research on Educational Standards and Student Testing, Graduate School of Education, University of California, 1989.

*Mary Lee Smith is professor of educational policy studies at Arizona State University.*

*This chapter provides a brief synthesis of the examples described in the four case study chapters, linking them to the framework outlined in Chapter One and the design types offered in Chapter Two.*

# Advances in Mixed-Method Evaluation: A Synthesis and Comment

*Leslie J. C. Riggin*

Mixed-method evaluations have advanced to the point of being obsolete as a distinct type of evaluation. Evaluators have learned that combining quantitative and qualitative information is not only advisable but inevitable. What experimental study does not rely on qualitative data to help rule out alternative plausible hypotheses? What evaluation based on participant observation does not consider the frequency with which a theme emerges? Is there a performance monitoring system that is not supplemented by telephone interviews or site visits when either surprisingly strong or undesirably low performance is reported? The need to argue for the interdependence of qualitative and quantitative methods is over.

The need for guidance on combining data from these different method types continues, however. This volume offers guidance on two fronts. First, with regard to the purpose of combining methods, Greene and Caracelli (Chapter One) propose using qualitative and quantitative methods together to develop a rich understanding of our evaluands and to generate new insights from the juxtaposition of paradigm elements. In other words, methods can be seen not only as sources of different kinds of information but also as carriers of different paradigm elements that—when combined—enable us to see our data in enriched and new ways. Greene and Caracelli contrast this dialectical position with (1) the pragmatic position, in which methods are mixed without consideration of paradigm issues to make an evaluation more responsive; and (2) the purist position, in which methods can be mixed, but paradigm elements are incompatible and thus cannot be combined.

The second front on which the volume offers guidance is in the craft of mixed-method evaluation design. Although most evaluations use both

New Directions for Evaluation, no. 74, Summer 1997 © Jossey-Bass Publishers

qualitative and quantitative data, it is less clear that evaluators are using systematic approaches when collecting and analyzing both types of data. Caracelli and Greene (Chapter Two) describe a range of approaches to designing mixed-method evaluations, from component designs that keep the data from the different method types separate, to integrated designs that bring the data together at the analysis or interpretation stages.

To reflect on the guidance that the editors provide in their chapters, this chapter first applies it to the examples described in Chapters Three through Six, and then comments on its potential for advancing our practice.

## Analysis of Examples of Mixed-Method Evaluations

The examples described in Chapters Three through Six demonstrate the variety of ways in which qualitative and quantitative methods are brought together in evaluation. But from what position on the relationship of paradigm and practice were these mixed-method evaluations conducted? Specifically, are methods brought together to juxtapose elements of different paradigms and then data in these integrated designs analyzed to develop a rich understanding of the evaluand and its context? Or are methods brought together for more practical and responsive rationales? Table 7.1 summarizes my analysis of the examples in relation to these questions. (Note that this analysis is limited by the amount of detail provided in the examples. Undoubtedly, some of my classifications would be different if I had more information on the evaluators' intent and procedures.)

**Relationship Between Paradigm and Practice.** The evaluations described in the chapters appear to illustrate either pragmatic or purist positions toward the mixing of methods. Datta (Chapter Three) takes an explicitly pragmatic approach, claiming that design decisions should be "practical, contextually responsive, and consequential." The H-2A Farmworkers Protection Evaluation that she describes used qualitative methods to answer a variety of background questions (such as the history of the program, the availability and quality of data) and a combination of qualitative and quantitative methods to answer questions about program effectiveness. Datta argues that this combination was (1) practical because plenty of resources were available, (2) contextually responsive because mixed methods provided information on causal processes that would not have been available from a single method alone, and (3) consequential in identifying fixable problems in agency processes. She does not describe a paradigmatic framework and emphasizes the practicality and responsiveness of the method choices.

Like Datta, Chen (Chapter Five) describes an essentially pragmatic approach to evaluation in which method choices are driven by the contingencies of the nature of information required, the availability of data, and the influence of the environment on the program. In Chen's two examples, the diverse methods were selected because contingencies required them and then used together to develop and evaluate a program theory. Although the theory-

## Table 7.1. Summary of Evaluation Examples

| Example of Evaluation Programs (Chapter) | How Mixed Methods Are Used in Relation to Paradigm | Design Type |
|---|---|---|
| Indonesian Child Survival Evaluation (Chapter Three) | To address limited time and data resources without (explicit) regard for paradigm. | Component—Expansion |
| H-2A Farmworkers Protection Evaluation (Chapter Three) | To answer a variety of questions about compliance, process, and effects without (explicit) regard for paradigm. | Component—Complementarity |
| USDA Personnel Management Demonstration Project (Chapter Four) | To develop methods and strengthen causal inference within "a predominantly quantitative framework." | Integrated—Embedded: Qualitative methods are analyzed in the framework established by the experimental design. |
| Garbage-Reduction Program (Chapter Five) | Contingencies require mixed methods. | Component—Expansion |
| Anti–Drug Abuse Program (Chapter Five) | Contingencies require mixed methods. | Integrated—Holistic: Data from different methods are examined together in the framework of program theory. |
| Arizona Student Assessment Program (Chapter Six) | Used in congruence with mental model's emphasis on data's comprehensiveness. | Integrated—Holistic: Data from different sources are interpreted together through a common analytic approach. |

driven approach provides a framework for designing and analyzing mixed-method evaluations, the methods are selected without regard to their paradigm attributes.

In contrast to Datta and Chen, the Chapter Four authors—Mark, Feller, and Button—claim an explicit paradigmatic framework for their evaluation of the USDA Personnel Management Demonstration Project. Their framework of emergent realism embraces features that have traditionally been associated with different paradigms (such as understanding local contexts and analyzing regularities across contexts). Although they describe how their combination of methods allows dialectical insights to emerge, their rationale for mixing methods is essentially pragmatic, specifically their point that understanding complex social phenomena requires a mixture of approaches. At the same time, an argument can be made that this evaluation illustrates a purist position: the emergent realist framework is not advocating combining paradigms. Despite embracing different methods and evaluation foci traditionally associated with different paradigms, Mark, Feller, and Button distinguish emergent realism from constructivism in terms of its stance on the nature of reality, and from positivism in terms of its stance on the ability to make claims of knowledge.

While the evaluations in Chapters Three and Five seem to illustrate a pragmatic position toward the relationship of paradigm and mixed-method practice, and while the evaluation in Chapter Four can be multiply classified, Smith's evaluation of the Arizona Student Assessment Program (ASAP) in Chapter Six appears to illustrate a purist stance in which mixing paradigm elements is neither sensible nor feasible. In introducing the ASAP evaluation, Smith dismisses the centrality of paradigms, focusing instead on the role our mental models play in determining our practice. Although mental models may or may not line up with a paradigm, the mental model she describes as guiding her evaluation of ASAP seems consistent with the interpretivist paradigm. The ASAP evaluation combined methods to increase the evaluation's comprehensiveness and narrative value (as well as to build credibility with some of the audiences), thus both achieving paradigmatic coherence and meeting contextual demands.

The argument for the ASAP evaluation as an illustration of the purist position lies in the characterization of one's crude mental model as the product of "disciplinary, cultural, historical, social, and ideological roots," rather than the explicit product of a logical process. If mental models are differentiated from paradigms in part by their inherent nature, and if mental models drive our evaluation choices, then all of the examples would be illustrations of the purist stance. Thus, just as the USDA evaluation is catholic in its approach because emergent realism demands a variety of kinds of information, the evaluations that Datta and Chen describe are eclectic in their approaches because the evaluators' mental models place a high priority on practicality and responsiveness. In other words, the evaluators are selecting mixed methods because they are consistent with their mental models, not to develop tensions across potentially inconsistent paradigm attributes. Despite the argument that all of these evaluations could be defined as purist, the purist classification seems to fit the ASAP evaluation best because the other authors describe their evaluation choices as the result of logical frameworks, rather than as the result of more fixed mental models.

**Elements of Different Paradigms.** Because none of the evaluations appears to have had an explicitly dialectical relationship between paradigm and practice, Table 7.1 has no column for the elements of different paradigms that were combined. However, each evaluation had a combination of characteristics that are associated with, but not necessarily inherent to, different paradigms. For example, the ethnographic case studies in the H-2A Farmworkers Protection Evaluation provided a microlevel perspective within two counties that helped the evaluators understand the patterns found in the macrolevel analysis of employment and wage data (Chapter Three). In the USDA demonstration project, mixed methods brought together information about how personnel officers experienced new hiring practices, and data on the causal relationship between the hiring practices and various intended outcomes (Chapter Four). Similarly, the anti–drug abuse evaluation obtained qualitative data from the teachers' perspectives to help explain patterns in quantitative data on the level and prevalence of teacher satisfaction (Chapter Five). The ASAP evaluation used a survey to examine the breadth of certain responses to the assessment program that were also explored in rich detail through case studies (Chapter Six). Certainly, these examples demonstrate the obvious statement that different kinds of methods are useful for obtaining different kinds of information. Yet, nothing suggests that these combinations of method types were selected because they brought together aspects of different paradigms.

**Design Choices.** Both component and integrated designs are illustrated in the evaluation examples. Lacking a paradigmatic or integrative framework, the evaluations that Datta describes are easily classified as component designs. The Indonesian Child Survival Evaluation illustrates an expansion design, using quantitative data to answer questions about trends over time and qualitative data to answer questions about implementation patterns. The H-2A Farmworkers Protection Evaluation provides an example of a complementarity design: quantitative data on employment and wages complement the ethnographic case studies, providing different perspectives on the same question. While these classifications seem best, given the information provided, alternative classifications could be made. For example, if it had not lost staff resources at the critical analysis and interpretation stage, the H-2A evaluation might have become integrated through iterations of analysis (in which the microlevel data on the program's context informed analysis of the macrolevel data on employment, and analysis of the macrolevel data prompted further analysis of the ethnographic data, and so on).

Despite the program theory framework of the garbage-reduction evaluation, Chen classifies it as a component design for expansion purposes because "different methods were used for different program theory domains and evaluation questions." In this case, resources were sufficient and the evaluation questions were such that integration was not required. In contrast, the contingencies of the anti–drug abuse evaluation involved bringing different methods together, each sacrificing some rigor in order to achieve multiple requirements with limited resources. The limitations that the methods would have had on their own were overcome when the evaluators analyzed the data within a program theory framework that maximized the methods' utility, despite trade-offs in quality. The integrating theoretical framework defines this evaluation as holistic in its design.

The USDA personnel evaluation includes features of component designs (such as mixing methods for triangulation), but appears to be primarily an embedded integrated design. The qualitative data were analyzed and interpreted within the framework of the experimental design, which provided information on causal processes and the limits of generalizability. The design also included some iteration of qualitative and quantitative methods in the development and later refinement of the survey instrument.

The ASAP evaluation also includes elements of more than one integrated design type. As with the USDA evaluation, the quantitative survey was based on analyses of qualitative data, illustrating an iterative design. Then all data were analyzed separately before being analyzed together and holistically integrated in the development and critical examination of a set of assertions.

**Summary of the Analysis.** Although all the evaluations mix methods and characteristics that are traditionally associated with different paradigms, none can be considered intentionally dialectical. The Indonesian Child Survival, H-2A Farmworkers Protection, Garbage-Reduction, and Anti–Drug Abuse evaluations illustrate the pragmatic stance in which paradigms are acknowledged and respected but are not central to the selection of methods. In contrast, the USDA Personnel Management Demonstration Project selected mixed methods for practical reasons within a paradigm that embraces both methods and other features traditionally associated with different paradigms. The ASAP evaluation used mixed methods because they were consistent with the evaluator's mental model. Both the USDA demonstration project and the ASAP evaluations can be considered examples of a purist approach in that they are conducted within a set of assumptions about how to develop and justify claims of knowledge and do not acknowledge a need to incorporate elements of differing paradigms.

## Reflections on the Guidance for Mixed-Method Evaluation

The evaluations discussed above exemplify purposeful mixed-method practice. Yet, at first glance, they do not seem to illustrate the "balanced, reciprocal relationship between philosophy and methodology" advanced by Greene and Caracelli (Chapter One). The proposal to balance philosophy and methodology assumes that qualitative and quantitative methods, while not inherent to a paradigm, can act as carriers of paradigm attributes and should be selected for that ability (Greene and Caracelli). The examples in this volume certainly use mixed methods to combine characteristics traditionally associated with different paradigms. Moreover, the combination of these characteristics created rich understandings of the evaluands. Consider the H-2A Farmworkers Protection Evaluation: without the ethnographic fieldwork in the two counties, the employment and wage data would have been woefully incomplete. In the case of the ASAP evaluation, the survey enabled the discovery of how responses to ASAP were distributed across the state's teachers and administrators. In addition, as Mark, Feller, and Button point out, combining these different features provides the opportunity for new insights to emerge, even though such insights cannot be brought about by planning alone.

Thus, evaluations can be strengthened by combining different characteristics, and mixing methods is one of the ways in which different characteristics can be incorporated. But the evaluators do not seem to have considered paradigm attributes in their selection of methods. Neither the characteristics nor the methods seem inherently or even importantly linked to paradigms.

Fortunately, the advance in mixed-method practice outlined by Greene and Caracelli in Chapter One does not depend on the idea of mixing paradigms so much as on the counterpoint of contrasting concerns and perspectives. As the examples demonstrate, it is the combining of disparate elements that develops a thorough understanding of the phenomenon and creates the opportunity to see our data in new ways. Mixing methods is one of the vehicles for achieving this counterpoint, whether the contrapuntal features are linked to paradigms or not. In fact, the examples' lack of consideration for the paradigmatic connections of the features they combine suggests that the hope expressed in Chapter One—that mixed-method evaluation can move the paradigm debates beyond irreconcilable differences—has been achieved. We have advanced so far beyond those debates that characteristics of formerly antagonistic schools of thought are combined in evaluation as a matter of course.

The variety of design options provides further evidence that the value of combining features formerly associated with different paradigms has been recognized. Caracelli and Greene provide a typology of these designs in Chapter Two, which includes some subtle distinctions. For example, although both of Chen's evaluations used an integrating framework of program theory, the garbage-reduction example is classified as component and the anti–drug abuse example is identified as integrated. The difference lies in the interdependence of the data at the analysis stage. Similarly, the USDA personnel demonstration and the ASAP evaluations are classified differently, the former as an embedded design and the latter as a holistic design, although both evaluations use a single integrative framework to interpret different types of data. Where the USDA personnel demonstration evaluation used qualitative data in a somewhat subordinate, supporting role within the experimental framework, the ASAP evaluation interpreted the qualitative and quantitative data together, using a single analytic approach. These distinctions, while fine, are important in describing the degree of synthesis obtained in evaluations that mix methods with the purpose of combining dissimilar perspectives.

Equally important is the lesson we learn from applying the design options to the examples in Chapters Three through Six—that is, that a variety of approaches can be used in a single evaluation, selected with attention to both contextual constraints (such as the time available for analysis and interpretation, the expectations of the audiences, and the skills of the evaluators) and coherence with a paradigm or mental model. Thus, for example, the Indonesian Child Survival Evaluation used several data sources and combined them in at least two component designs—expansion and complementarity. The USDA personnel demonstration evaluation provides the most varied example, with triangulation, iterative, and embedded designs used at different points. As with the classifications outlined in Chapter Two, the variety of design options employed in practice supports the conclusion that combinations of features traditionally associated with different paradigms are becoming routine.

## Advances in Mixed-Method Evaluation Revisited

The editors of this volume encourage evaluators to become more articulate about our means of and goals for combining method types. They have provided us with terms to use in describing our designs and ways to think about combining methods to generate new insights. As the evaluations described in the chapters amply illustrate, we are beyond paradigm debates about irreconcilable differences. We have recognized that while we may hold differing views about the nature of reality and the warrants for a claim of knowledge, we share a respect for developing rich information about programs by using different methods and perspectives.

LESLIE J. C. RIGGIN is assistant professor of program evaluation in The Florida State University's Department of Educational Research.

# Index

# ORDERING INFORMATION

NEW DIRECTIONS FOR EVALUATION is a series of paperback books that presents the latest techniques and procedures for conducting useful evaluation studies of all types of programs. Books in the series are published quarterly in Spring, Summer, Fall, and Winter and are available for purchase by subscription as well as by single copy.

SUBSCRIPTIONS cost $63.00 for individuals (a savings of 28 percent over single-copy prices) and $105.00 for institutions, agencies, and libraries. Please do not send institutional checks for personal subscriptions. Standing orders are accepted. Prices subject to change. (For subscriptions outside of North America, add $7.00 for shipping via surface mail or $25.00 for air mail. Orders *must be prepaid* in U.S. dollars by check drawn on a U.S. bank or charged to VISA, MasterCard, or American Express.)

SINGLE COPIES cost $22.00 plus shipping (see below) when payment accompanies order. California, New Jersey, New York, and Washington, D.C., residents please include appropriate sales tax. Canadian residents add GST and any local taxes. Billed orders will be charged shipping and handling. No billed shipments to post office boxes. (Orders from outside North America *must be prepaid* in U.S. dollars by check drawn on a U.S. bank or charged to VISA, MasterCard, or American Express.)

SHIPPING (SINGLE COPIES ONLY): $50.00 and under, add $4.50; to $75.00, add $5.50; to $100.00, add $6.50; to $150.00, add $7.50; over $150.00, add $8.50.

DISCOUNTS FOR QUANTITY ORDERS are available. Please write to the address below for information.

ALL ORDERS must include either the name of an individual or an official purchase order number. Please submit your order as follows:
Subscriptions: specify series and year subscription is to begin
Single copies: include individual title code (such as PE59)

MAIL ALL ORDERS TO:
Jossey-Bass Publishers
350 Sansome Street
San Francisco, California 94104-1342

FOR SUBSCRIPTION SALES OUTSIDE OF THE UNITED STATES, CONTACT
any international subscription agency or Jossey-Bass directly.